Marie Barber's 515 Inspirational Cross-Stitch Designs

Sterling Publishing Co., Inc. New York
A Sterling/Chapelle Book

Chapelle

Owner	Staff	Photography
Jo Packham	Ann Bear, Areta Bingham,	Kevin Dilley/Hazen Photography
	Kass Burchett, Rebecca Christensen,	
Editor	Holly Fuller, Marilyn Goff,	Photostylist
Karmen Quinney	Holly Hollingsworth, Shawn Hsu,	Jo Packham
	Susan Jorgensen, Pauline Locke,	
	Barbara Milburn, Linda Orton,	
	Leslie Ridenour, Cindy Stoeckl	

 We would like to offer our sincere appreciation for the valuable support given in this ever changing industry of new ideas, concepts, designs, and products. Several projects shown in this publication were created with outstanding and innonative products developed by DMC Floss, Kreinik, Mill Hill Beads, Wichelt Fabric, and Zweigart Fabric.

Library of Congress Cataloging-in-Publication Data

Barber, Marie.
    Marie Barber's 515 inspirational cross stitch designs / Marie Barber.
       p.   cm.
    "A Sterling/Chapelle book."
    Includes index.
    ISBN 0-8069-6255-0
    1. Cross-stitch—Patterns   2. Christian art and symbolism.
I. Title.   II. Title: 515 inspirational cross stitch designs.
III. Title: Five hundred fifteen inspirational cross stitch designs.
TT778.C76B383   1999   98–46796
746.44'3041—dc21   CIP

10 9 8 7 6 5 4 3 2 1

First paperback edition published in 2000 by
Sterling Publishing Company, Inc.
387 Park Avenue South, New York, N.Y. 10016
© 1999 by Chapelle Ltd.
Distributed in Canada by Sterling Publishing
c/o Canadian Manda Group, One Atlantic Avenue, Suite 105
Toronto, Ontario, Canada M6K 3E7
Distributed in Great Britain and Europe by Cassell PLC
Wellington House, 125 Strand, London WC2R 0BB, England
Distributed in Australia by Capricorn Link (Australia) Pty Ltd.
P.O. Box 6651, Baulkham Hills, Business Centre, NSW 2153, Australia
Printed in China
All rights reserved

Sterling ISBN 0-8069-6255-0 Trade
                  0-8069-5598-8 Paper

If you have any questions or comments, please contact: Chapelle Ltd., Inc., P.O. Box 9252 Ogden, UT 84409 (801) 621-2777 • FAX (801) 621-2788 • E-mail Chapelle1@ aol.com

Quote on page 37 was taken from *The Velveteen Rabbit* by Margery Williams.

About the Author

Marie Barber, born and raised in Kristianstad, Sweden, now lives in Ragland, Alabama, on the Coosa River with her husband and their two children.

Marie says she has always loved to draw and illustrate. At the age of 14, she was the youngest student to study oil painting under the instruction of the late Dr. Göran Trönnberg.

She came to the United States in 1983 as an exchange student, and in 1987, returned after being accepted to the Art Institute of Atlanta. She has freelanced as a novel illustrator for a Swedish weekly publication and her artwork is featured at Loretta Goodwin's Gallery in Birmingham, Alabama. Although she has explored several avenues of the art world, Marie says she found her passion in 1993 when she began designing cross-stitch patterns.

Table of Contents

General Instructions

Introduction

Contained in this book are 515 counted cross-stitch designs.

Each page of graphed designs has its own color code. To create one-of-a-kind motifs, vary colors in graphed designs.

Fabric for Cross-stitch

Counted cross-stitch is worked on even-weave fabrics. These fabrics are manufactured specifically for counted-thread embroidery, and are woven with the same number of vertical as horizontal threads per inch.

Because the number of threads in the fabric is equal in each direction, each stitch will be the same size. The number of threads per inch in even-weave fabrics determines the size of a finished design.

Number of Strands

The number of strands used per stitch varies, depending on the fabric used. Generally, the rule to follow for cross-stitching is three strands on Aida 11, two strands on Aida 14, one or two strands on Aida 18 (depending on desired thick-ness of stitches), and one strand on Hardanger 22.

For backstitching, use one strand on all fabrics. When completing a french knot, use two strands and one wrap on all fabrics, unless otherwise directed.

Finished Design Size

To determine size of finished design, divide stitch count by number of threads per inch of fabric. When design is stitched over two threads, divide stitch count by half the threads per inch. For example, if a design with a stitch count of 120 width and 250 length were stitched on a 28 count linen over two threads, the end size would be 8⅝" x 17⅞".

Preparing Fabric

Cut fabric at least 3" larger on all sides than finished design size to ensure enough space for desired assembly.

To prevent fraying, whipstitch or machine-zigzag along raw edges or apply liquid fray preventive.

Needles for Cross-stitch

Blunt needles should slip easily through fabric holes without piercing fabric threads. For fabric with 11 or fewer threads per inch, use a tapestry needle size 24; for 14 threads per inch, use a tapestry needle size 24 or 26; for 18 or more threads per inch, use a tapestry needle size 26. Never leave needle in design area of fabric. It may leave rust or a permanent impression on fabric.

Floss

All numbers and color names on the codes represent the DMC brand of floss. Use 18" lengths of floss. For best coverage, separate strands and dampen with a wet sponge. Then put together the number of strands required for fabric used.

Centering the Design

Fold the fabric in half horizontally, then vertically. Place a pin in the fold point to mark the center. Locate the center of the design on the graph. To help in centering the designs, arrows are provided at left-side center and bottom center. Begin stitching all designs at the center point of graph and fabric.

Securing the Floss

Insert needle up from the underside of the fabric at starting point. Hold 1" of thread behind the fabric and stitch over it, securing with the first few stitches. To finish thread, run under four or more stitches on the back of the design. Never knot floss, unless working on clothing.

Another method of securing floss is the waste knot. Knot floss and insert needle down from the right top side of the fabric about 1" from design area. Work several stitches over the thread to secure. Cut off the knot later.

Carrying Floss

To carry floss, weave floss under the previously worked stitches on the back. Do not carry thread across any fabric that is not or will not be stitched. Loose threads, especially dark ones, will show through the fabric.

Cleaning the Finished Design

When stitching is finished, soak fabric in cold water with a mild soap for five to ten minutes. Rinse well and roll in a towel to remove excess water. Do not wring. Place work face down on a dry towel and iron on warm setting until the fabric is dry.

Cross-stitch (X st)

Stitches are done in a row or, if necessary, one at a time in an area.

1. Insert needle up between woven threads at A.

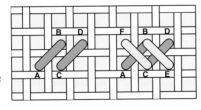

2. Go down at B, the opening diagonally across from A.

3. Come up at C and down at D, etc.

4. To complete the top stitches creating an "X", come up at E and go down at B, come up at C and go down at F, etc. All top stitches should lie in the same direction.

Backstitch (BS)

1. Insert needle up between woven threads at A.

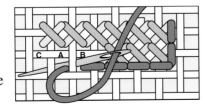

2. Go down at B, one opening to the right.

3. Come up at C.

4. Go down at A, one opening to the right.

French Knot (FK)

1. Insert needle up between woven threads at A, using one strand of embroidery floss.

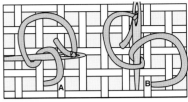

2. Loosely wrap floss once around needle.

3. Go down at B, the opening across from A. Pull floss taut as needle is pushed down through fabric.

4. Carry floss across back of work between knots.

Lazy Daisy Stitch (LD)

1. Insert needle up between woven threads at A.

2. Go down at B, using same opening as A.

3. Come up at C, crossing under two threads. Pull through, holding floss under needle to form loop.

4. Go down at D, crossing one thread.

Long Stitch (LS)

1. Insert needle up between woven threads at A.

2. Go down at B, crossing two threads. Pull flat.
Repeat A–B for each stitch. Stitch may be horizontal, verticle, or diagonal as indicated in examples 1, 2, and 3. The length of the stitch should be the same as the length indicated on the graph.

Satin Stitch (SS)

1. Insert needle up between woven threads at A.

2. Go down at B, forming a straight stitch.

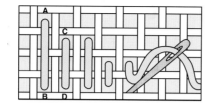

3. Come up at C and go down at D, forming another smooth straight stitch that is slightly overlapping the first.

4. Repeat to fill design area.

Bead Attachment (Bds), Crystal Treasure (CT), and Glass Treasure (GT)

Beads and treasures should sit facing the same direction as the top cross-stitch.

1. Make first half of a cross-stitch.

2. Insert needle up between woven threads at A.

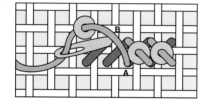

3. Thread one bead before going down at B, the opening diagonally across from A.

4. To strengthen stitch, come up again at A and either go through bead again or split threads to lay around bead and go down at B again.

Working with Different Cross-stitch Elements

Depending on the type of elements used to create a cross-stitch piece, the same cross-stitch design can have several different looks. Use silk floss, overdyed floss, metallic thread, and beads to add dimension and texture to your projects.

The photo on the facing page features the same cross-stitch design that has been completed with four different elements: floss, overdyed floss, silk floss, and beads. The wreath graph and four codes representing the different elements can be found on page 10. *Note: The different codes have been provided for the wreath only. However, the different elements can be applied on any cross-stitch piece. Kreinik Conversion Chart can be found on pages 126-127.*

Silk Thread Tips

• Strands should be 12–15" in length.

• Color variation between skeins and bleeding of thread onto fabrics is common with silk thread.

• Silk thread can be combined with cotton thread in the same piece.

• When using variegated strands, cross each stitch as it is made rather than crossing the stitch on the way back across a row.

• Silk cross-stitched pieces should be dry-cleaned rather than hand-washed.

Thread Descriptions

Embroidery Floss is a stranded cotton and the most versatile thread available. **Overdyed Floss** is Egyptian cotton, overdyed by hand, creating a subtle shaded effect. **Rachel** ribbon is a tubular, nylon thread with a shimmery look. **Waterlillies** floss is a 12-ply hand-dyed silk with a subtle sheen look.

The threads listed above are distributed by **Anchor**, 30 Patewood Drive, Greenville, SC 29615; **DMC Corporation**, 10 Port Kearny, South Kearny, NJ 07032; **Kreinik Manufacturing Company Inc.**, 3106 Timanus Lane, Suite #101, Baltimore, MD 21244; **Needle Necessities, Inc.**, 14746 N.E. 95 St., Redmond, WA 98052; **The Caron Collection**, 67 Poland St., Bridgeport, CT 06605.

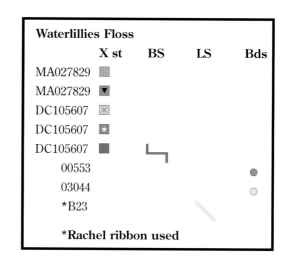

DMC Floss

	X st	BS	LS	Bds
472	▨			
471	▼			
3348	⊠			
3347	★			
3346	▧			
00553				●
03044				○
*B23				

*Rachel ribbon used

Waterlillies Floss

	X st	BS	LS	Bds
MA027829	▨			
MA027829	▼			
DC105607	⊠			
DC105607	★			
DC105607	▧			
00553				●
03044				○
*B23				

*Rachel ribbon used

Kreinik Silk Floss

	X st	BS	LS	Bds
2112	▨			
2114	▼			
2121	⊠			
2123	★			
2124	▧			
00553	☐			●
03044	☐			○
*B23	☐			

*Rachel ribbon used

Mill Hill Beads

	Bds	LS
00525	▨	
00167	▼	
00341	⊠	
02020	★	
00332	▧	
00553	●	
03044	○	
*B23		

*Rachel ribbon used

Stitch Count: 36 x 42

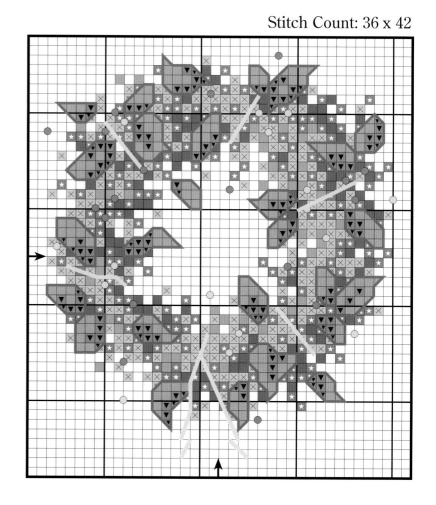

To Be Friends

Stitch Count: 40 x 21

Stitch Count: 32 x 17

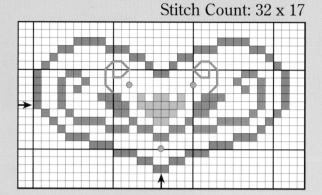

Stitch Count: 50 x 38

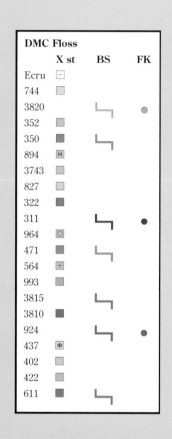

DMC Floss			
	X st	BS	FK
Ecru	−		
744			
3820		⌐	●
352			
350		⌐	
894	H		
3743			
827			
322			
311		⌐	●
964	○		
471		⌐	
564	+		
993			
3815		⌐	
3810			
924		⌐	●
437	✳		
402			
422			
611		⌐	

Stitch Count: 17 x 23

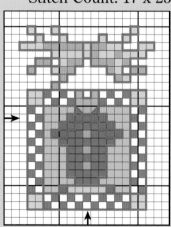

Stitch Count: 20 x 23

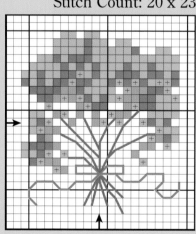

Stitch Count: 26 x 29

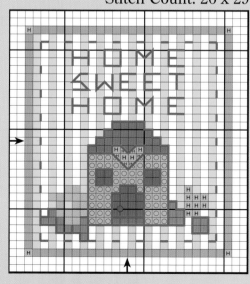

Stitch Count: 30 x 49

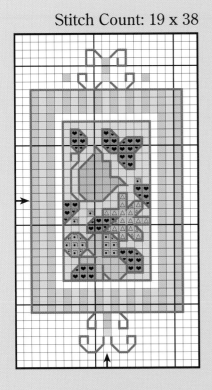

Stitch Count: 16 x 18

Stitch Count: 17 x 17

Stitch Count: 10 x 18

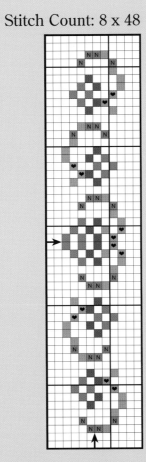

Stitch Count: 19 x 10

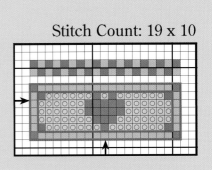

Stitch Count: 19 x 38

Stitch Count: 8 x 48

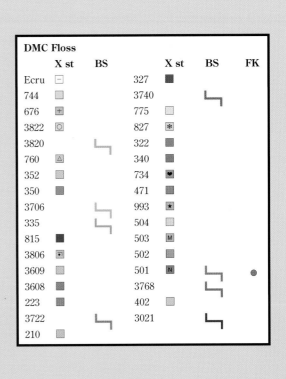

DMC Floss							
	X st	**BS**			**X st**	**BS**	**FK**
Ecru	−			327	■		
744	□			3740		⌐	
676	+			775	□		
3822	○			827	✳		
3820		⌐		322	■		
760	△			340	■		
352	□			734	♥		
350	■			471	■		
3706		⌐		993	★		
335		⌐		504	□		
815	■			503	M		
3806	·			502	■		
3609	□			501	N	⌐	●
3608	■			3768		⌐	
223	■			402	□		
3722		⌐		3021		⌐	
210	□						

Stitch Count: 40 x 55

Stitch Count: 29 x 30

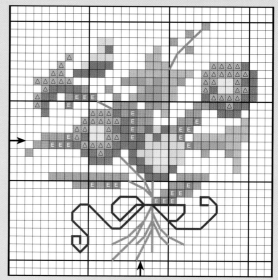

Stitch Count: 31 x 20

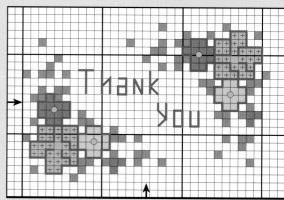

Stitch Count: 80 x 24

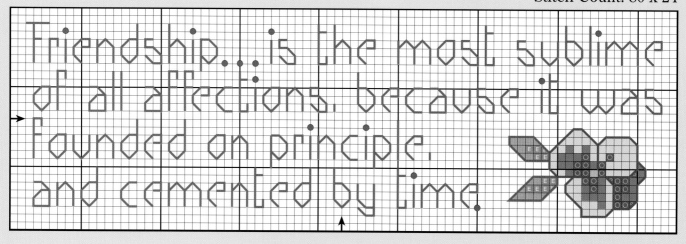

DMC Floss														
	X st	FK		X st	BS		X st	BS	FK		X st	BS	FK		X st	BS	CT
712	☐		3354	△		3747	☐			472	▦			924	▧	
676	▦	●	223	▦		340	▦			471	E	⌐		613	▦	⌐
729	▦		3803	▦	⌐	3807	★			989	▦			420		⌐
761	☐		210	▦		792	◙	⌐	●	320	▪	⌐		12209		
760	✚		550	▦	⌐	791		⌐		501	▦	⌐	●			●

14

Stitch Count: 26 x 29

Stitch Count: 47 x 18

Stitch Count: 46 x 8

Stitch Count: 50 x 33

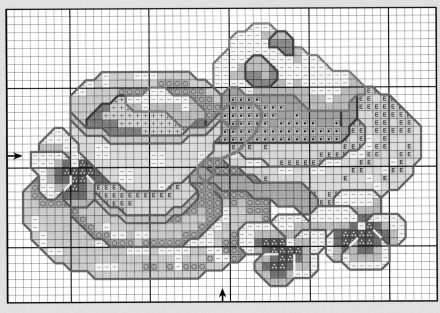

Stitch Count: 22 x 36

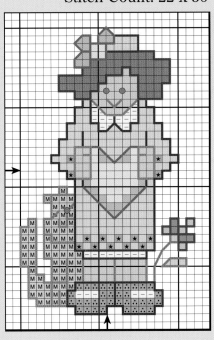

Stitch Count: 15 x 23

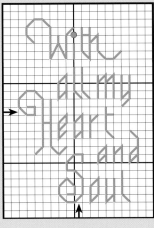

DMC Floss									
	X st	BS	FK		X st	BS	FK		X st	BS	FK
Ecru	□		○	3803			●	3815		
744				815				924		
3822				3743				3364		
3820	★			775				3363		
676	⊡			827	E			402		
729				341				437	+	
945				340	⊡			436	M	
352				322				435		
350			●	793				801		
3689				792				644		
3806				504				611		●
3608				503	◎			3021		

15

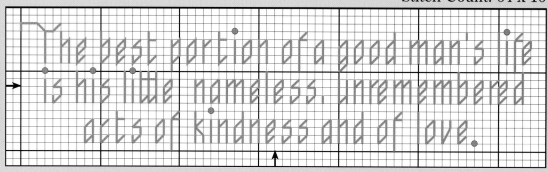

Stitch Count: 28 x 48

Stitch Count: 9 x 26

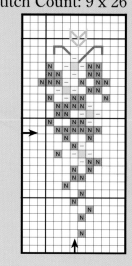

Stitch Count: 21 x 11

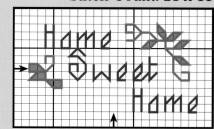

Stitch Count: 25 x 14

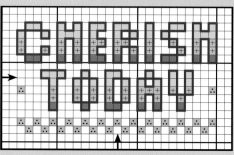

Stitch Count: 11 x 11

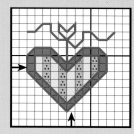

Stitch Count: 21 x 25

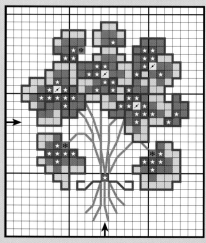

DMC Floss											
	X st	BS		X st	BS		X st	BS	FK	LS	
Ecru	⊟		3747	⊡		3816	◩	⌐	●		
3078	⁄		340	◼		3815		⌐			
744	▦		3807	✶	⌐	3768		⌐			
676	△		775	▦		3363	✳	⌐			
729	◼		827	⊞		402	▦				
3713	▦		322	◼		437	▦				
760	⁙	⌐	311	◼	⌐	435	◼				
350	◼	⌐	504	▦		801	◼		⌐		
3743	▦		503	N							

Stitch Count: 62 x 8

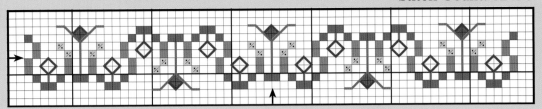

Stitch Count: 37 x 52

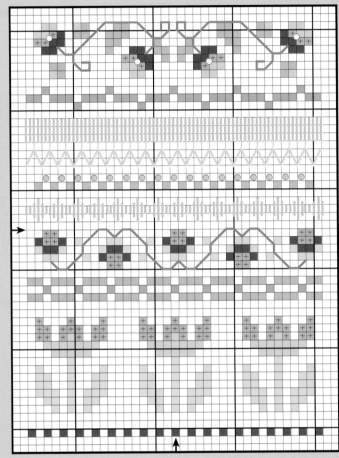

DMC Floss

	X st	BS	FK	LS	SS	Bds
760	+					
776						
894	○					
893	N					
309						
3722		⌐				
3687						
3685		⌐				
3755						
772						
3348	⅍					
3347						
3346		⌐				
3363		⌐				
996	⊡					
3817						
3816	⊡					
3815		⌐	●			
924		⌐				
00123						○
02003						●
*MA115823					‖‖	

*Overdyed floss used

Stitch Count: 24 x 23

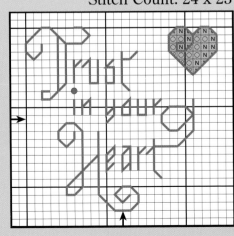

Stitch Count: 32 x 28

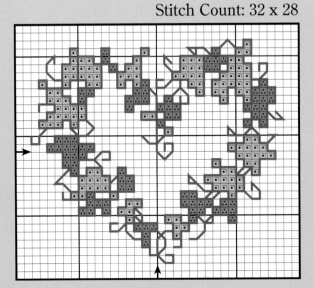

Stitch Count: 38 x 39

Stitch Count: 28 x 14

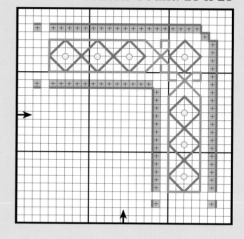

Stitch Count: 23 x 23

Stitch Count: 16 x 26

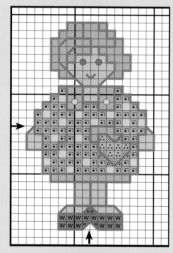

DMC Floss												
	X st	BS	FK		X st	BS			X st	BS	FK	Bds
Ecru	☐			3325	▨			436	▨			
727	▨		○	932	△			422	▨			
676	+			959	▣			612	W			
3821	▨			3813	▨			611	▨		●	
3045	▨	⌐		502	Z			3781	▨	⌐		
951	▨			3768	▨	⌐		844	▨	⌐		
945	◩			924	▨	⌐		3022	▨	⌐		
760	▨			471	▨	⌐		3787	■			
351	▨			739	☐			3021	▨	⌐		
349	▨	⌐		437	H			00123				○
221	▨	⌐	●									

Stitch Count: 16 x 16

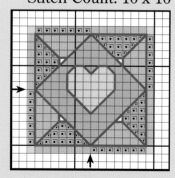

Stitch Count: 53 x 21

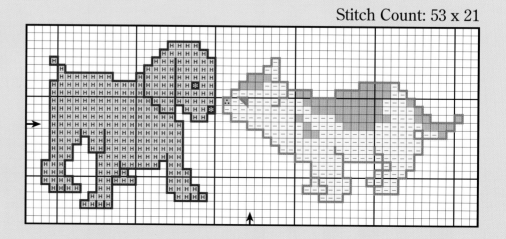

Stitch Count: 32 x 45

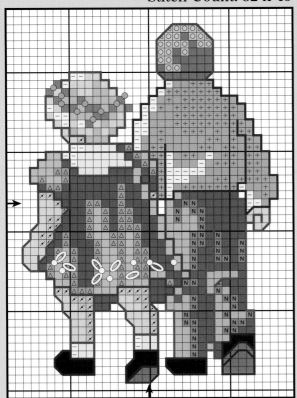

Stitch Count: 27 x 28

Stitch Count: 22 x 58

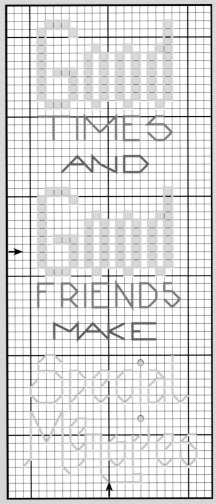

Stitch Count: 45 x 5

DMC Floss							
	X st	BS	FK	LD	X st	BS	FK
Ecru			○	⬭	471		
727					3363	⌐	
3821					3813		
951					502	N	
945					958	⌐	
760	✳				3810	⌐	
893		⌐	●		3768		
352					924	⌐	
351	△		●		739		⌐
349					436	○	
221		⌐			435		
3743					356		●
3041		⌐			3022		
341					3787	■	
3325					3781		⌐
932	+				844		⌐
3348							

Stitch Count: 45 x 14

Like trees in the forest our friendship shall endure.

Stitch Count: 25 x 11

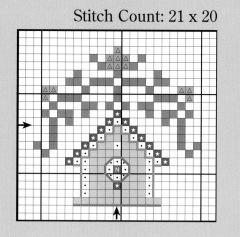

Stitch Count: 48 x 10

Stitch Count: 21 x 20

Stitch Count: 40 x 3

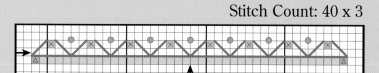

Stitch Count: 38 x 53

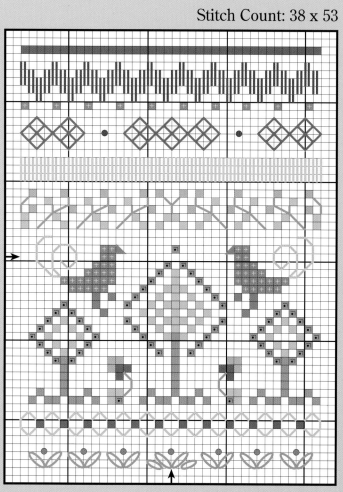

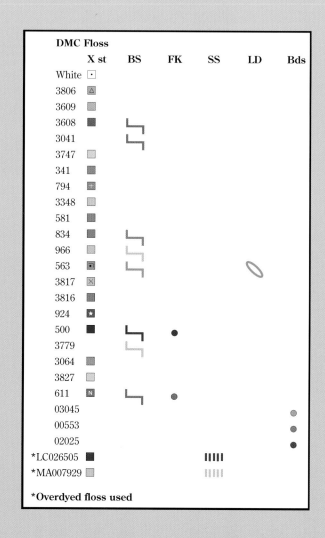

DMC Floss						
	X st	BS	FK	SS	LD	Bds
White	·					
3806	△					
3609						
3608		⌐				
3041		⌐				
3747						
341						
794	+					
3348						
581						
834		⌐				
966		⌐				
563	·	⌐				O
3817	X					
3816						
924	★					
500		⌐	●			
3779		⌐				
3064						
3827						
611	N	⌐	●			
03045						●
00553						●
02025						●
*LC026505				‖‖‖		
*MA007929				‖‖‖		
*Overdyed floss used						

20

Stitch Count: 18 x 19

Stitch Count: 37 x 41

Stitch Count: 38 x 13

Stitch Count: 38 x 53

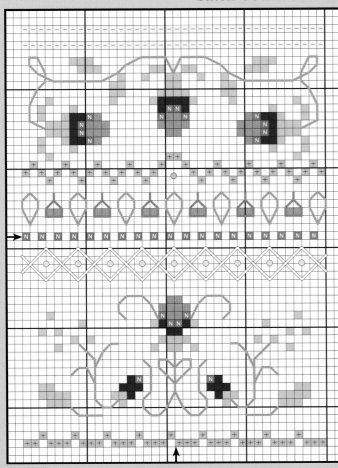

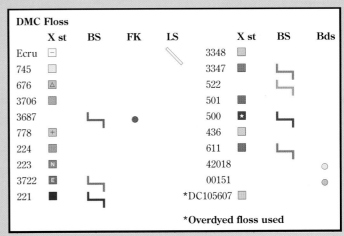

DMC Floss								
	X st	BS	FK	LS		X st	BS	Bds
Ecru	⊟			/	3348			
745					3347			
676	△				522		⌐	
3706					501			
3687		⌐	●		500	★	⌐	
778	+				436			
224					611		⌐	
223	N				42018			○
3722	E	⌐			00151			●
221	■	⌐			*DC105607			
					*Overdyed floss used			

Stitch Count: 27 x 27

DMC Floss

	X st	BS	FK		X st	BS	LD
Ecru	⊟	⌐		772	▢		
727	▢			704	▨		
3821	⊞		○	471	Z		⬭
951	▢			987	▨		
945	◩			3813	▨		
963	◎			563	▨		
760	⊠			964	K		
3706	⛶			959	✳		
894	▨			958	▨		
893	E			3810	▨		
352	▨			502	▨		
351	△		○	501	N	⌐	
349	■		●	3768	★		
3722		⌐		924		⌐	
221		⌐		739	▢		
327		⌐	●	436	▨		
3325	▨			435	▨		
932	▣			3781		⌐	

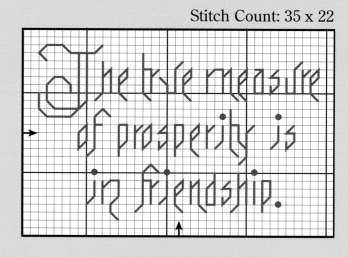

Stitch Count: 35 x 22

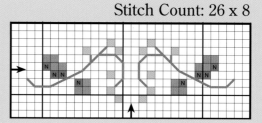

Stitch Count: 26 x 8

Stitch Count: 7 x 59

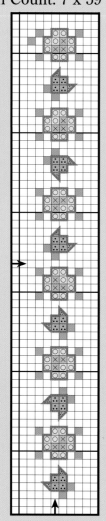

Stitch Count: 58 x 58

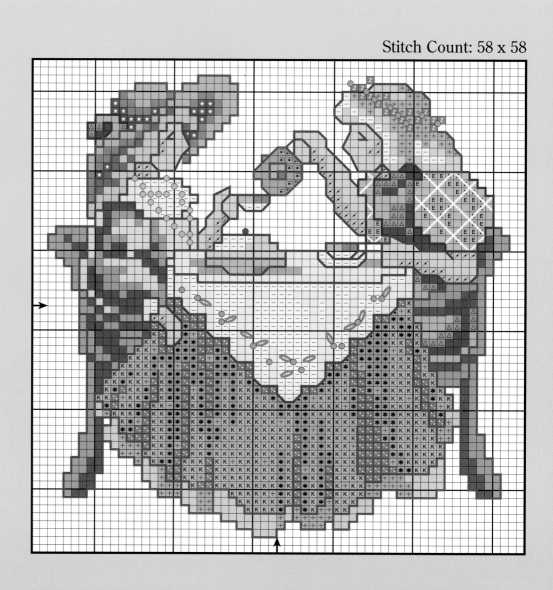

22

To Have Faith

To every thing
there is a season,
and a time
to every purpose
under the heaven.

Eccl. 3:1

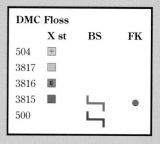

DMC Floss

	X st	BS	FK
504			
3817			
3816	E		
3815			
500			

Stitch Count: 9 x 57

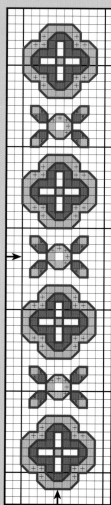

Stitch Count: 66 x 10

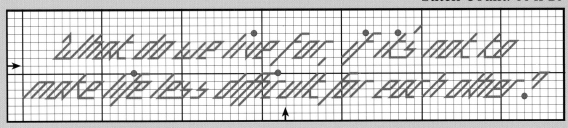

Stitch Count: 40 x 54

Stitch Count: 22 x 38

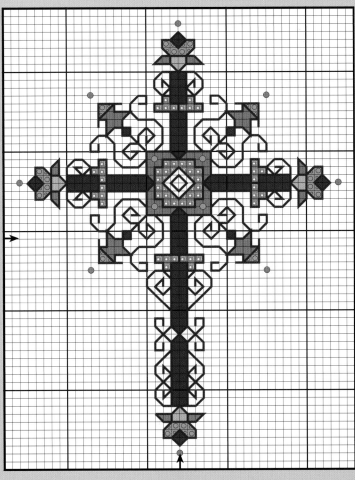

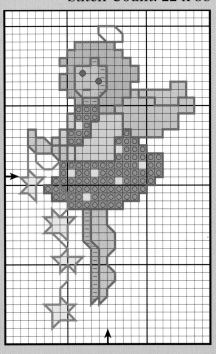

Stitch Count: 34 x 19

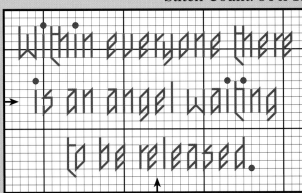

DMC Floss			
	X st	BS	FK
445			
676			
945			
758			
3041		⌐	
747			
813			
797			
3807		⌐	●
336		⌐	
772			
993			
3813			
3816			●
3815		⌐	●
3828		⌐	
611		⌐	●

MARK 11:9

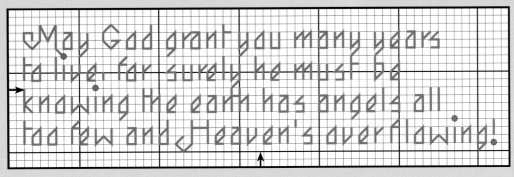

Code for Pages 26-27

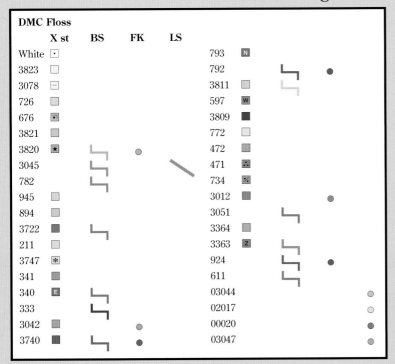

DMC Floss

	X st	BS	FK	LS				
White					793			
3823					792			
3078					3811			
726					597			
676					3809			
3821					772			
3820					472			
3045					471			
782					734			
945					3012			
894					3051			
3722					3364			
211					3363			
3747					924			
341					611			
340					03044			
333					02017			
3042					00020			
3740					03047			

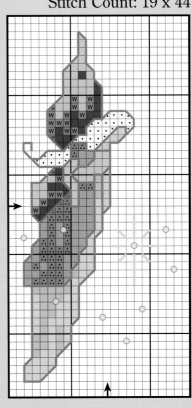

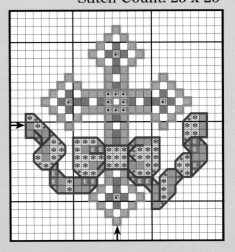

God is my strength and power:
and he maketh my way perfect.
2 SAMUEL 22:33

Stitch Count: 35 x 20

Stitch Count: 17 x 23

Stitch Count: 13 x 10

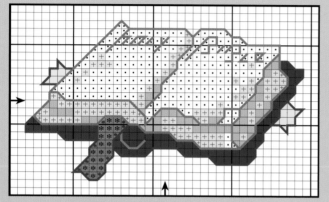

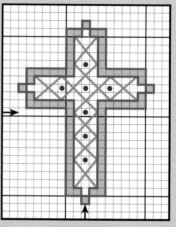

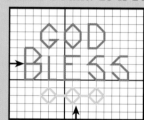

Stitch Count: 33 x 51

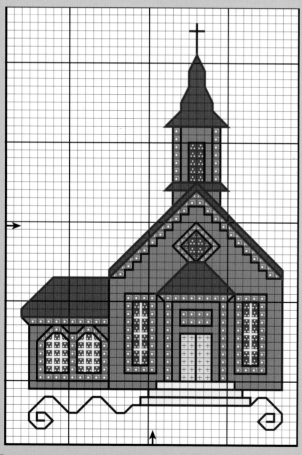

Stitch Count: 34 x 10

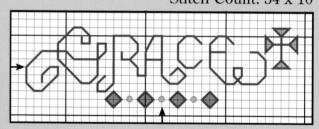

DMC Floss								
	X st	BS	FK	LS		X st	BS	Bds
White	·				794	✳		
445					3807	■		
746		⌐			792			
745	+				930	▦		
3821					3827			
3046					834	▣		
3045				/	420			
3722					356	■		
221			•		3787			
341					03042			•
519			•					

Stitch Count: 19 x 28

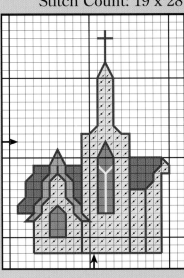

Stitch Count: 24 x 34

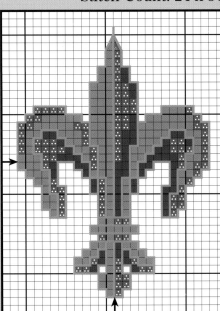

Stitch Count: 18 x 14

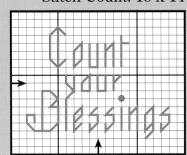

Stitch Count: 24 x 14

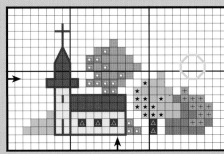

Stitch Count: 28 x 15

Stitch Count: 6 x 30

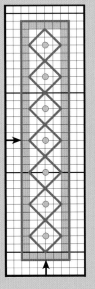

Stitch Count: 22 x 16

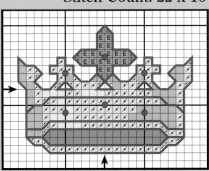

Stitch Count: 25 x 35

DMC Floss							
	X st	BS	FK		X st	BS	FK	Bds
3823				472			
745				471			
3821				3817			
729				3815			
3727	E			3827			
223				437			
3740				356			
794				839			
793				613			
792				611			
3364				3021			
3363				03053			
3819				02015			

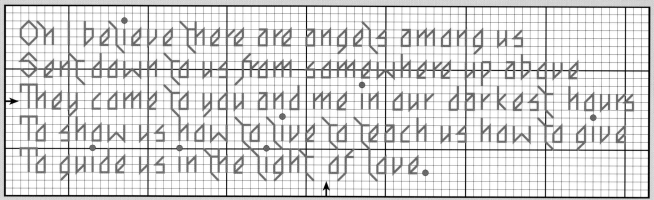

Oh I believe there are angels among us
Sent down to us from somewhere up above
They come to you and me in our darkest hours
To show us how to live to teach us how to give
To guide us in the light of love.

Stitch Count: 38 x 45

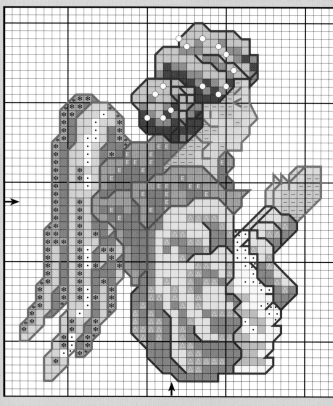

Stitch Count: 26 x 28

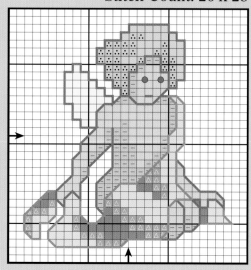

Stitch Count: 12 x 32

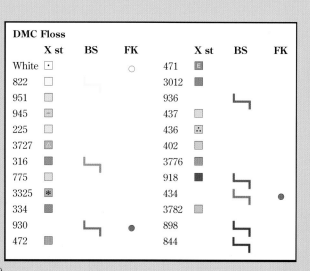

Stitch Count: 16 x 27

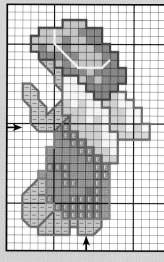

DMC Floss						
	X st	BS	FK		X st	BS	FK
White	⊡		○	471	E		
822	☐			3012	▦		
951	☐			936		⌐	
945	⊟			437	☐		
225	☐			436	⊡		
3727	△			402	☐		
316	▦	⌐		3776	▦		
775	☐			918	■	⌐	
3325	✳			434		⌐	●
334	▦	⌐		3782	☐		
930		⌐	●	898		⌐	
472	▦			844		⌐	

Stitch Count: 40 x 40

Stitch Count: 19 x 13

Stitch Count: 24 x 24

Stitch Count: 22 x 35

Stitch Count: 40 x 12

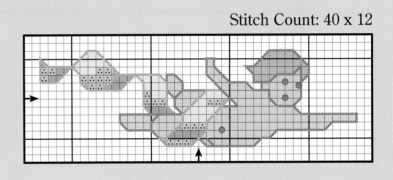

DMC Floss								
	X st	**BS**		**X st**	**BS**		**X st**	**BS**	**FK**
White	⊡		3803	■		471	▣	
727	▢		747	✳		3051		⌐
725	▼		3761	▢		734	✴	
676	+		813	▨		832	▨	
783	▨		334	◙		422	▢	
945	▢		793	⊞		869		⌐
758	−		336		⌐	3826	▨	
352	△		369	▢		611		⌐	●
963	▢		368	▢		801		⌐
894	⣿		3363	▨				
335	▨	⌐	520	▼				

31

Stitch Count: 26 x 18

Stitch Count: 18 x 17

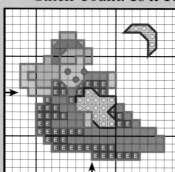

Stitch Count: 18 x 22

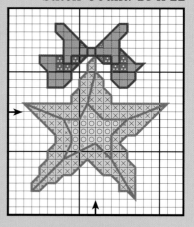

Stitch Count: 16 x 30

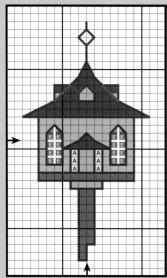

Stitch Count: 55 x 30

Stitch Count: 25 x 34

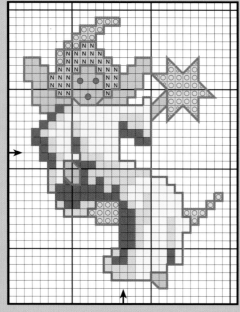

DMC Floss

	X st	BS		X st	BS	FK		X st	BS	FK
Ecru	⊟		3803	■			3827	N		
3823	A		3608	■			422	▣		
676	▦		718		⌐		3826	★		
744	○		554	▦			434	■		
725	⊠		333	■	⌐		433		⌐	
783	▦		775	▦			611		⌐	●
945	▦		794	▦			839	■	⌐	●
819	☐		793	E			3024	▦		
894	+	⌐	3363	▦	⌐	●	3023	▽		
221		⌐	993	▦			3021		⌐	
3689	▦		943	▨						

Stitch Count: 40 x 23

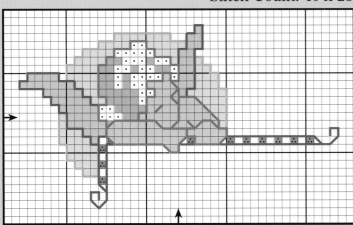

Stitch Count: 22 x 23

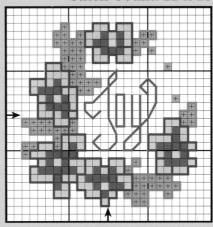

Stitch Count: 54 x 12

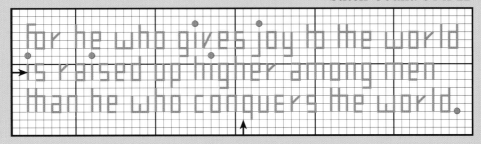

Stitch Count: 13 x 13

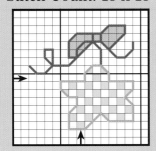

Stitch Count: 41 x 28

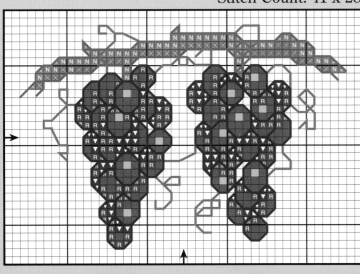

DMC Floss

	X st	BS	FK
White	⊡		
727	☐		
3820		⌐	
945	☐		
211	☐		
3740		⌐	
3747	☐		
341	▦		
340	■		
3746	R		
792	▼		
791		⌐	
470		⌐	
3364	✛		
3363		⌐	
3816		⌐	
3782	☐		
356		⌐	●
3828	N		
420	✕		
869	■		
611		⌐	

Stitch Count: 31 x 40

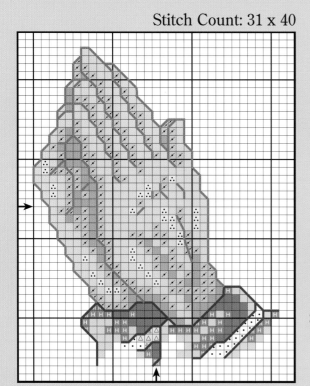

Stitch Count: 20 x 29

Stitch Count: 9 x 55

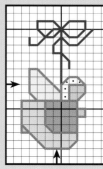

Stitch Count: 9 x 17

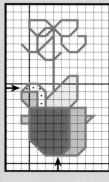

Stitch Count: 9 x 16

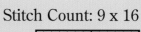

Stitch Count: 36 x 51

DMC Floss								
	X st	BS	FK		X st	BS	FK	Bds
White	·			747	−			
3823				813	H			
445			○	322				
676	+			311		⌐		
3822	★			564				
3821				993	E			
3770	∷			501		⌐	●	
951				3810		⌐		
945	✓			739	△			
3773				437	◎			
3772		⌐		435				
3712		⌐		434	▼			
221		⌐		433		⌐		
3747				420		⌐		
327		⌐		680	A			
3753				611		⌐		
931				3021		⌐		
3761				02011				●

To Comfort

Stitch Count: 23 x 28

Stitch Count: 24 x 27

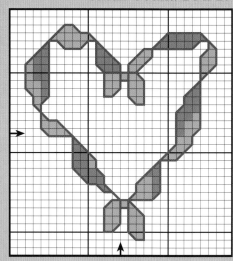

Stitch Count: 54 x 35

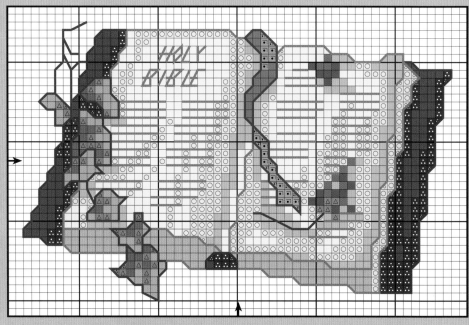

DMC Floss				
	X st	BS	FK	LS
White	·			
746				
3823	–			
727				
677	○			
676				
945				
352	⅔			
3706			●	
3731				
3803		⌐		
209				
3746				
747				
775	+			
519	✳			
598	▪			
597				
3807	★			
368				
502	△			
501				
500		⌐		
3808		⌐		
3364	E			
422				
420		⌐		
437	N			
435				
356		⌐	●	
611		⌐		
3781				
3031	▪	⌐		

Stitch Count: 67 x 13

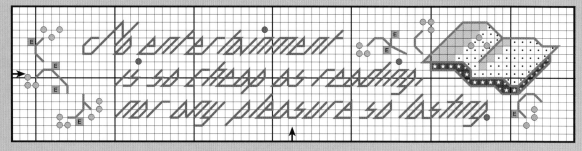

Stitch Count: 28 x 14

Stitch Count: 45 x 8

Stitch Count: 13 x 25

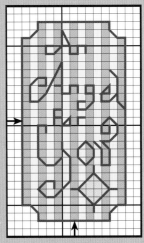

DMC Floss

	X st	FK	LS		X st	BS	FK		X st	BS	LS
White	·		╱	3721		⌐	●	563	·		
3078	☐			3727	··			504	☐		
3047	☐			316	■			503	+		
3045	★			3685		⌐		501		⌐	
951	☐			800	☐			926	■		
819	✎	○		3755	E			422	Z		
3716	■			334	■	⌐		420			╱
352	=			3750		⌐		3827	⊙		
3712	△			598	N			3830	■		
225	☐			959	■			842	■		
223	✳			772	☐			3781	■	⌐	

Stitch Count: 36 x 51

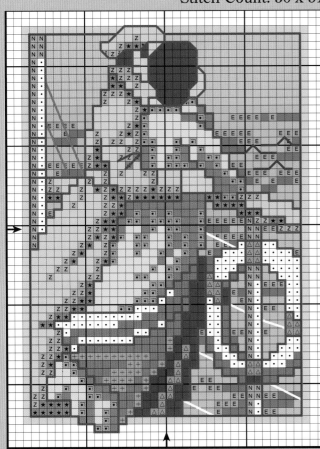

Stitch Count: 39 x 34

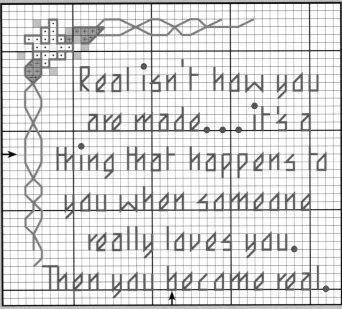

Real isn't how you are made... it's a thing that happens to you when someone really loves you. Then you become real.

Stitch Count: 72 x 13

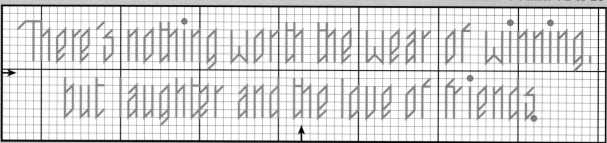

Stitch Count: 34 x 43

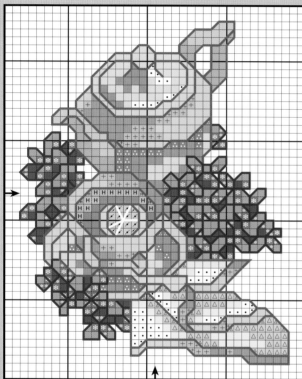

Stitch Count: 19 x 19

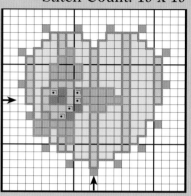

Stitch Count: 13 x 21

Stitch Count: 16 x 15

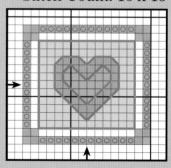

Stitch Count: 24 x 13

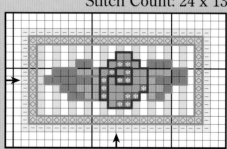

Stitch Count: 16 x 15

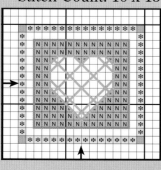

DMC Floss

	X st	BS	FK		X st	BS		X st	BS
White	·	⌐		327	■		369		
712	−			550		⌐	368	+	
3822				3041		⌐	502		
3820				341	E		739		
307	✳			800	◇		738	△	
727				3761			3827	✎	
3825				3325	N		977	H	
3340				813			976		
894				322	⁑		611		⌐
893	⊡			472			3781		⌐
3722		⌐	●	3051		⌐	3072		
554				3364	◎		648		
553	✳			3363		⌐	645		⌐

38

Stitch Count: 48 x 7

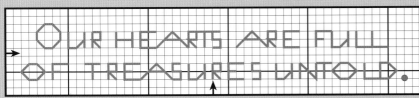

Stitch Count: 17 x 29

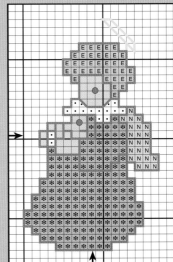

Stitch Count: 10 x 38

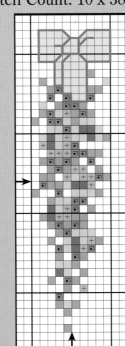

Stitch Count: 28 x 29

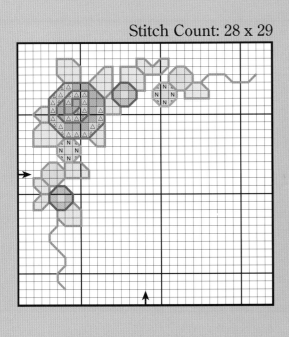

Stitch Count: 18 x 14

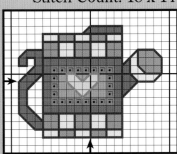

Stitch Count: 42 x 42

DMC Floss

	X st	BS		X st	BS	FK
White	·		3325	S		
712	☐		799	▦	⌐	
727	☐	⌐	798	★		
951	☐		797		⌐	
352	✳		772	☐		
776	△		3363		⌐	
899	▦		472	▦		
309		⌐	471	▪		
3688	▦		470	▦	⌐	
3803		⌐	937		⌐	
211	☐		3810		⌐	●
210	+		437	☐		
3041	▦	⌐	436	E		
3747	N	⌐	611		⌐	●
341	▦	⌐	3021		⌐	
775	☐					

Stitch Count: 66 x 4

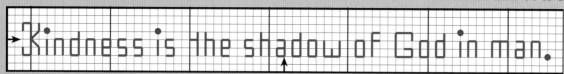

Stitch Count: 41 x 52

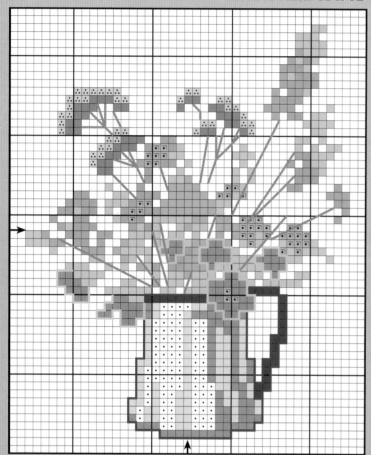

DMC Floss				
	X st	**BS**	**FK**	**Bds**
White	·			
Ecru	–			
445				
775				
3325	+			
3807		⌐	●	
3819				
580		⌐		
504	◎			
3817				
3816	E			
500		⌐		
436	M			
611		⌐	●	
762				
415				
317				
03055				●
*MA027829				
*MA036802				
*MA053901				
*MA0311001				
*LC026505				
*DC105607		⌐		
*MA1211013		⌐		
*Overdyed floss used				

Stitch Count: 59 x 4

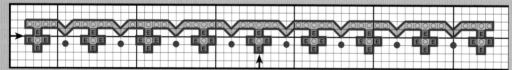

Stitch Count: 63 x 14

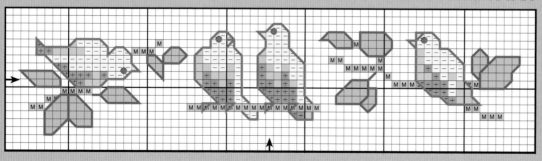

Stitch Count: 21 x 12

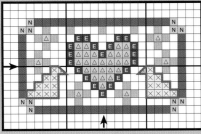

Stitch Count: 16 x 29

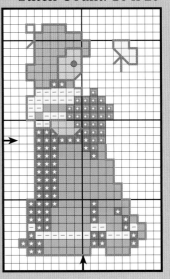

Stitch Count: 49 x 93

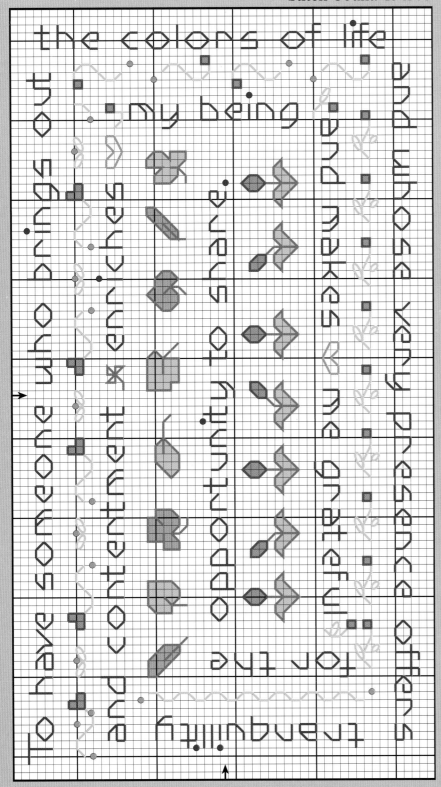

DMC Floss				
	X st	**BS**	**FK**	**LD**
Ecru	⊟			
3823	⊠			
3822	△			
3078	☐			
3774	▨			
3350		⌐		
3743	▦			
3747	N			
340	▩			
519	▦			
518	★	⌐		
3807	E			
471	▦			
501		⌐		
422	▦			
611		⌐⌐	●	
840		⌐⌐		
*MA053901	▩		●	
*DC105607	▨	⌐		⬭
*MA1711013	▦			
*MA112718		⌐	●	
*Waterlillies floss used				

41

Stitch Count: 58 x 9   Stitch Count: 15 x 27

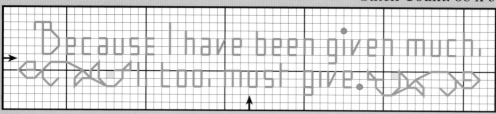

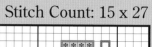

DMC Floss

	X st	BS	FK		X st	BS	FK
White	·			3348			
Ecru	−			471		⌐	
677				3364			
3822	✳			3363		⌐	
3774				992		⌐	
352	+			3816			
351				501	◎	⌐	
3705	△			924			
3689			○	437			
902		⌐		435	⊡		
554				977	N		
3740		⌐		3826			
3753	⋰			869	H		
747	E			3830	★		
827				611		⌐	
518		⌐	●	838	■	⌐	●
312		⌐					

Stitch Count: 32 x 17

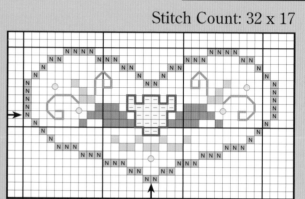

Stitch Count: 55 x 39   Stitch Count: 18 x 40

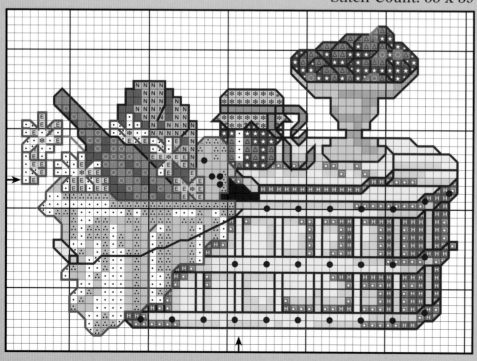

42

Stitch Count: 36 x 21

Stitch Count: 23 x 31

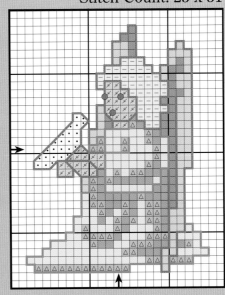

Stitch Count: 19 x 20

Stitch Count: 13 x 18

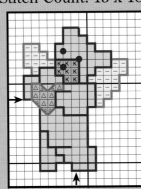

Stitch Count: 26 x 15

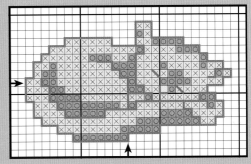

Stitch Count: 34 x 46

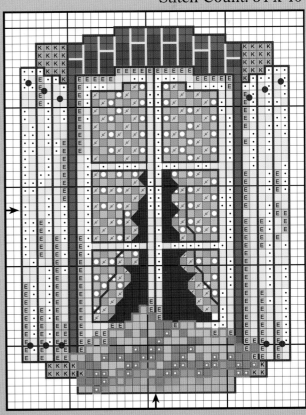

DMC Floss						
	X st	BS		X st	BS	FK
White	·		828			
712	×		3811	E		
3823	−		3807			
676			3819			
729			581			
3774	⨰		3011	▣		
950			739			
3713			437			
352	△		3827	+		
351			422	K		
350	○		3777			
223			3830	▨		
211			3782			
210	⠿		613	◎		
3041			611			●
3609			3021			●
3608			844	■		
341						

Stitch Count: 35 x 20

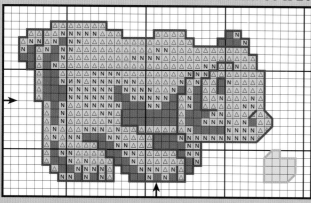

Stitch Count: 38 x 52

Adventure and excitement lie within

Stitch Count: 22 x 28

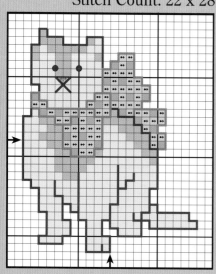

Stitch Count: 27 x 25

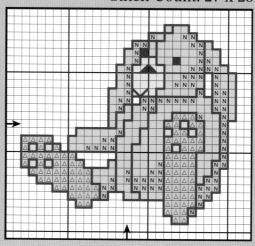

DMC Floss													
	X st	BS		X st	BS		X st	BS	LD		X st	BS	FK
White	·		963			3348				3776			
712			894	+	⌐	989			⬭	434			
744			3761	••		987	▼			420		⌐	
3820		⌐	519			437		⌐		869		⌐	
951			518	★	⌐	436	N			839		⌐	
945	%		959	⊙		3827	△			3024		⌐	
760			992	B		402	E			844		⌐	●
3712		⌐	924		⌐								

Stitch Count: 33 x 24

In the garden,
after a rainfall,
you can faintly, yes,
hear the breaking
of new blooms.

Stitch Count: 28 x 23

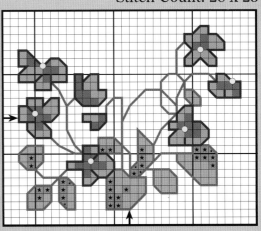

Stitch Count: 19 x 60

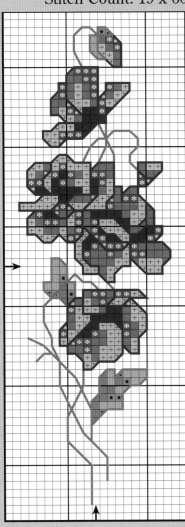

Stitch Count: 29 x 23

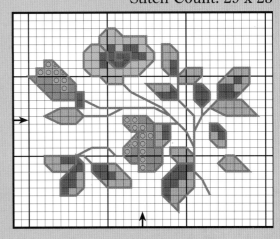

Stitch Count: 10 x 10

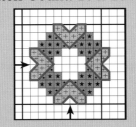

Stitch Count: 13 x 12

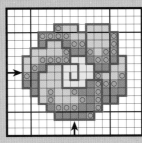

DMC Floss

	X st	BS	FK		X st	BS	FK
445	☐		○	3364	▩		
352	▨			3346	▪	⌐	
3706	◉			472	▨		
894	+			471	★		
891	▪			3011	▪		
335	▨			3051	▪	⌐	
321	✴			3827	☐		
814	■	⌐	●	356	▪		
3325	▨			611	▪	⌐	
322	▪	⌐		3031	■		
336		⌐	●				

Stitch Count: 72 x 5

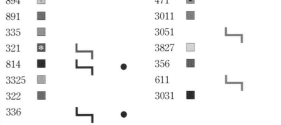

45

To Be Serene

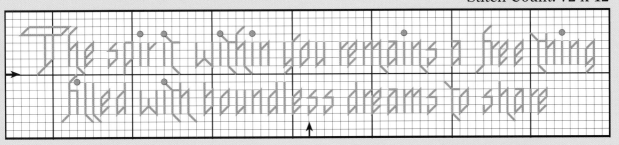

Stitch Count: 29 x 54

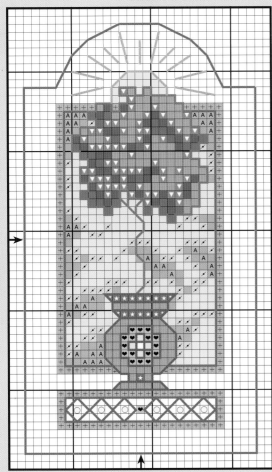

Stitch Count: 22 x 16

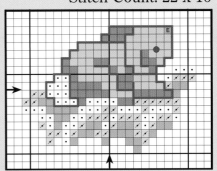

Stitch Count: 34 x 28

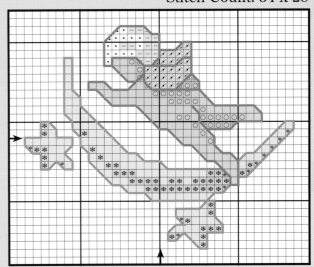

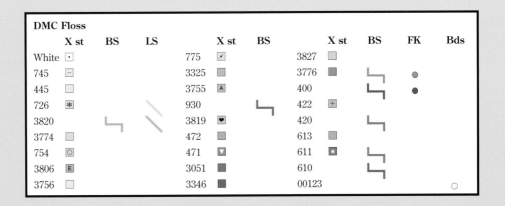

DMC Floss

	X st	BS	LS		X st	BS		X st	BS	FK	Bds
White	·			775	⟋		3827				
745	−			3325			3776		⌐	●	
445				3755	A		400			●	
726	✳	⌐	╱	930		⌐	422	+	⌐		
3820		⌐	╱	3819	♥	⌐	420				
3774				472			613				
754	○			471	▽		611	★	⌐		
3806	E			3051			610		⌐		
3756				3346			00123				○

Stitch Count: 44 x 4

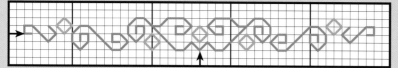

Stitch Count: 28 x 30

Stitch Count: 39 x 51

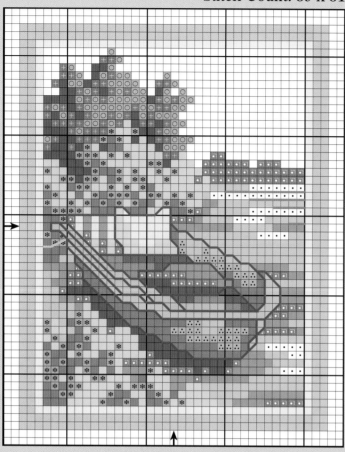

DMC Floss							
	X st	BS	FK		X st	BS	FK
White	·			3813	⊚		
3823				3816	+	⌐	
744				3815			
352				772			
223	△	⌐	●	368	✳		
3726				320		⌐	
341				472		⌐	
828				3364		⌐	
3325				3363		⌐	
813	⊡	⌐		3827			
930		⌐		437	E		
3811	⊡			3064			
992		⌐		356		⌐	●

Stitch Count: 76 x 5

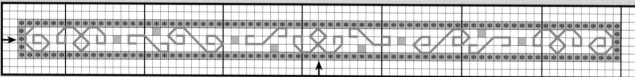

Stitch Count: 23 x 20

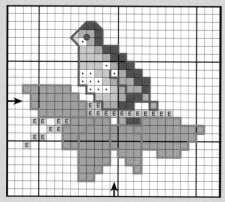

Stitch Count: 40 x 22

Stitch Count: 56 x 12

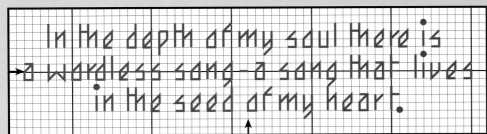

Stitch Count: 17 x 13

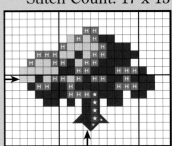

Stitch Count: 68 x 4

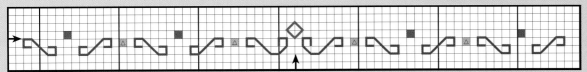

Stitch Count: 78 x 24

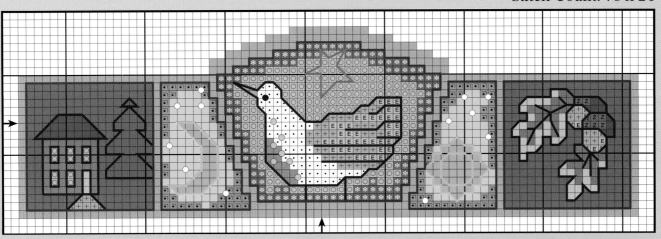

Stitch Count: 35 x 38

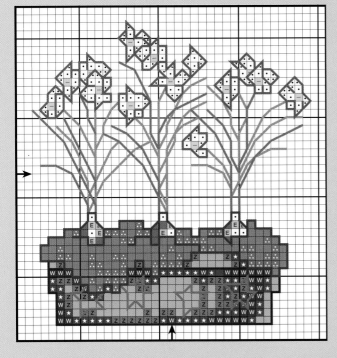

DMC Floss							
	X st	BS	FK		X st	BS	FK
White	·		○	370	▨		
726	–			581		⌐	
676	+			3051		⌐	
3821	▨			504	▨		
352	△			501	H		
351	▨			500	■		
224	▨			437	E		
3803		⌐	●	436		⌐	○
3746		⌐		435	▨		
747	▨			422	▨		
3766	⊡			356	▨	⌐	
792	▨	⌐		977	▨	⌐	
931	▨			976	Z	⌐	
3750		⌐		975	▨		
3811	○			918	W		
807	✳			301	★		
562	▨			300	■	⌐	
3348	▨			839		⌐	
3347	▨			838		⌐	●
372	▨						

Stitch Count: 40 x 53   Stitch Count: 2 x 44

Stitch Count: 23 x 36

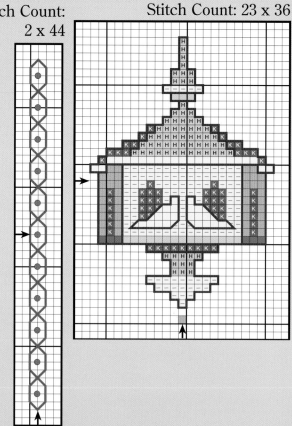

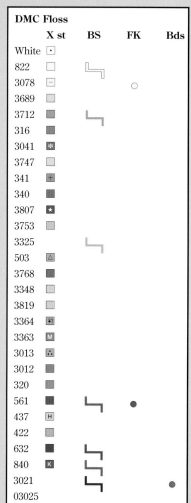

Stitch Count: 20 x 4

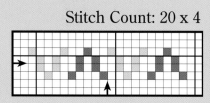

Stitch Count: 18 x 8

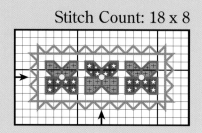

Stitch Count: 47 x 22

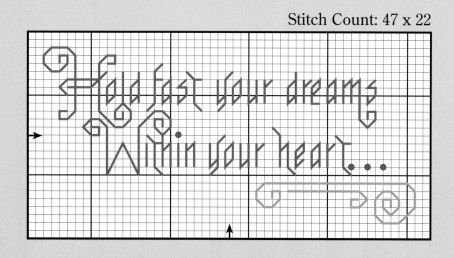

DMC Floss				
	X st	BS	FK	Bds
White	·			
822		⌐		
3078	—		○	
3689				
3712		⌐		
316				
3041	✻			
3747				
341	+			
340				
3807	✦			
3753				
3325		⌐		
503	△			
3768				
3348				
3819				
3364	▪			
3363	M			
3013	⋰			
3012				
320				
561		⌐	●	
437	H			
422				
632		⌐		
840	K	⌐		
3021		⌐		●
03025				

Stitch Count: 40 x 54

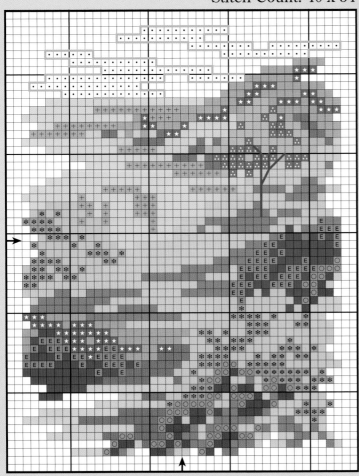

Stitch Count: 29 x 16

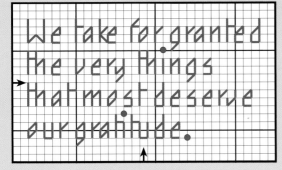

We take for granted the very things that most deserve our gratitude.

Stitch Count: 38 x 34

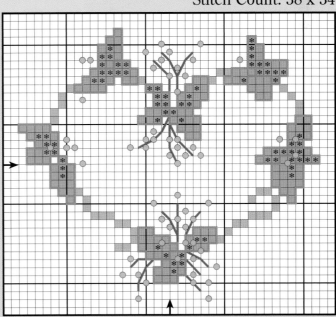

Stitch Count: 34 x 14

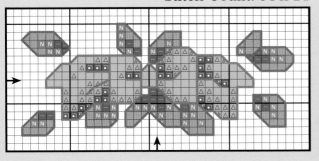

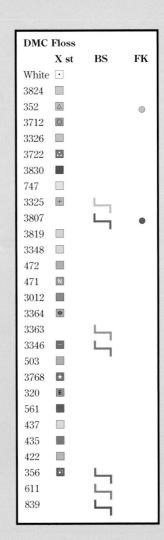

DMC Floss

	X st	BS	FK
White	·		
3824			
352	△		○
3712	◎		
3326			
3722	⊡		
3830			
747			
3325	+	⌐	
3807		⌐	●
3819			
3348			
472			
471	N		
3012			
3364	✳		
3363			
3346	⊞	⌐	
503			
3768	✶		
320	E		
561			
437			
435			
422			
356	⊡	⌐	
611		⌐	
839		⌐	

Stitch Count: 38 x 54

Stitch Count: 12 x 36

Stitch Count: 14 x 38

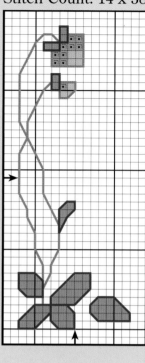

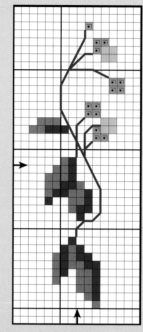

Stitch Count: 12 x 41

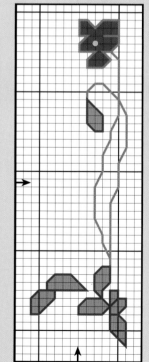

Stitch Count: 47 x 8

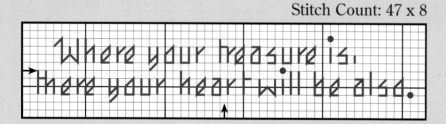

Where your treasure is, there your heart will be also.

Stitch Count: 19 x 18

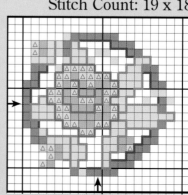

DMC Floss

	X st	BS	FK		X st	BS
676	▨		●	902		⌐
5282		⌐		3807	■	⌐
963	△			772	▢	
760	▨			581	▨	
3712	▣			3346	▦	
3705	▨			934		⌐
3722		⌐		3816	▨	
718	▨			501	▨	
3685		⌐	●	500	■	
341	▨			611		⌐

Stitch Count: 38 x 48

Stitch Count: 25 x 47

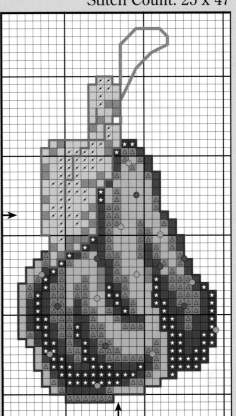

Stitch Count: 43 x 16

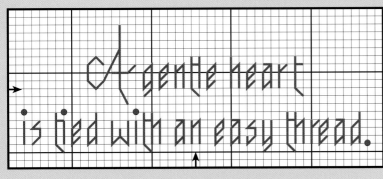

Stitch Count: 22 x 45

DMC Floss

	X st	BS	FK		X st	BS	Bds
782		⌐		561	■		
351	▦			500	★	⌐	
347	■			436	▦		
223	▦			434	▦	⌐	
3803	▦	⌐	●	355	▦		
902	■	⌐		05021			○
3348	▦			42027			○
372	▦			42029			○
369	▨			05086			●
368	▦			05555			○
320	▦			40556			●

Stitch Count: 32 x 24

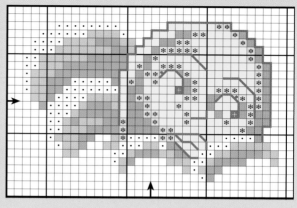

Stitch Count: 32 x 20

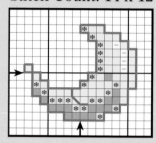

Stitch Count: 57 x 32

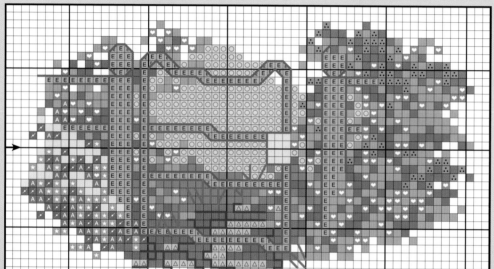

Stitch Count: 14 x 12

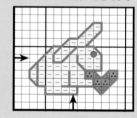

Stitch Count: 11 x 9

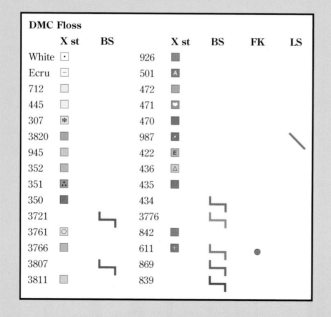

Stitch Count: 21 x 31

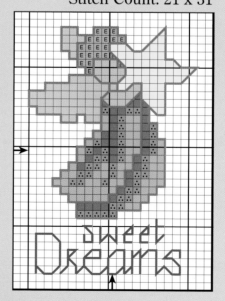

DMC Floss							
	X st	**BS**		**X st**	**BS**	**FK**	**LS**
White	·		926				
Ecru	−		501	A			
712			472				
445			471	♡			
307	✳		470				
3820			987				/
945			422	E			
352			436	△			
351			435				
350		⌐	434				
3721			3776				
3761	○	⌐	842				
3766			611	+		●	
3807		⌐	869				
3811			839				

Stitch Count: 40 x 19

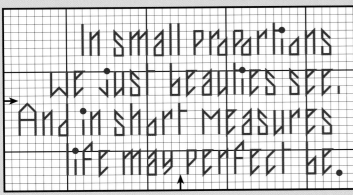

Stitch Count: 19 x 30

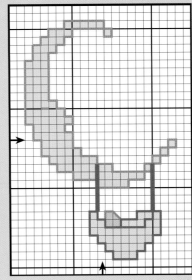

DMC Floss

	X st	BS	FK		X st	BS	LS	Bds
White	·			471	A			
745	+			470				
727				3011		⌐		
725	▽			924		⌐		
783		⌐		3827	◎			
781		⌐		3776	✳			
3045		⌐		611	▣	⌐		
945				3072				
963				648	✻			
747				646				
336		⌐	●	844		⌐		
472				02003				◯

Stitch Count: 25 x 17

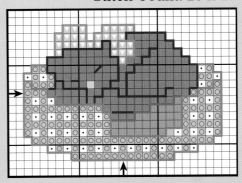

Stitch Count: 33 x 40

Stitch Count: 23 x 36

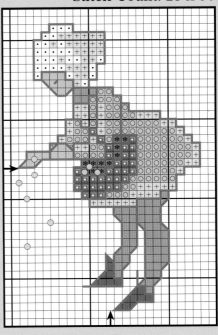

Stitch Count: 47 x 26

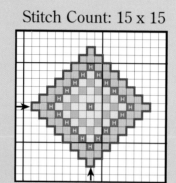

Stitch Count: 13 x 13

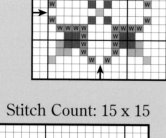

Stitch Count: 15 x 15

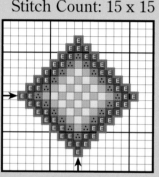

Stitch Count: 15 x 15

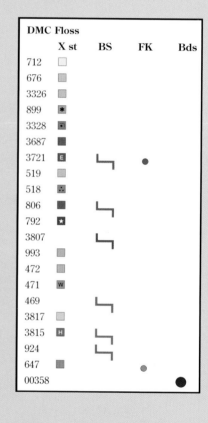

DMC Floss				
	X st	BS	FK	Bds
712				
676				
3326				
899	✳			
3328	⋅			
3687				
3721	E	⌐	●	
519				
518	⋅			
806		⌐		
792	★			
3807		⌐		
993				
472				
471	W			
469		⌐		
3817				
3815	H	⌐		
924		⌐		
647			●	
00358				●

Stitch Count: 44 x 44

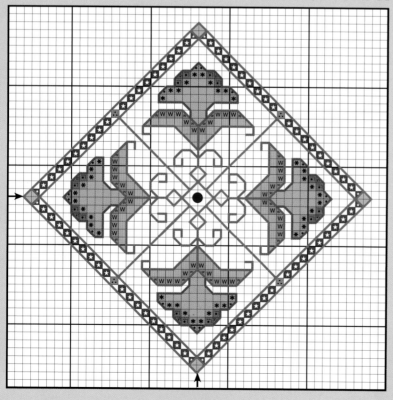

Stitch Count: 18 x 21

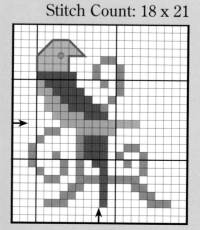

56

To Have Joy

Stitch Count: 26 x 31

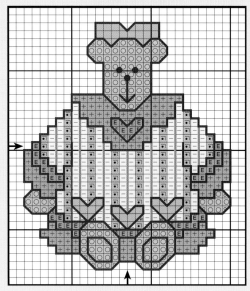

Stitch Count: 32 x 28

Stitch Count: 20 x 21

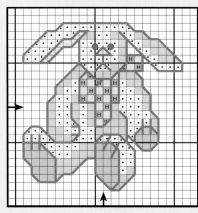

Stitch Count: 16 x 3

DMC Floss

	X st	BS	FK		X st	BS	FK
White	·			341	△		
Ecru	⊟			799		⌐	
445	☐			793	■		
729		⌐		772	☐		
945	☐			472	☐		
3824	⊡			3364	⋰		
3713	☐			993	N		
894	☐			959	E		
893	H			3815		⌐	
352	☐			3827	○		
351	◪			436	⁒		
3722		⌐	●	422	☐		
3041	■	⌐		839		⌐	●
828	☐			611		⌐	●
3325	⊞			3021		⌐	●

Stitch Count: 21 x 35

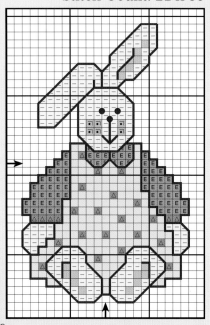

Stitch Count: 21 x 26

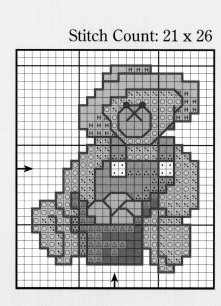

Stitch Count: 23 x 29

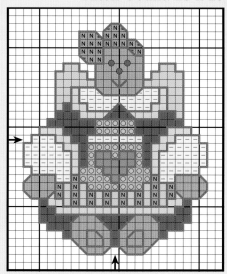

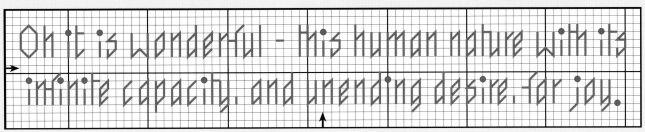

Stitch Count: 47 x 24

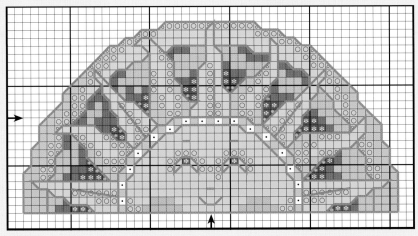

Stitch Count: 20 x 27

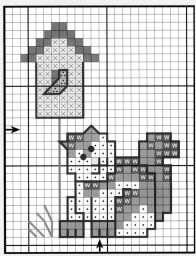

Stitch Count: 28 x 15

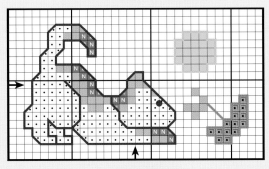

Stitch Count: 19 x 10

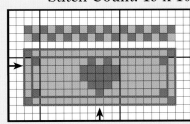

Stitch Count: 16 x 16

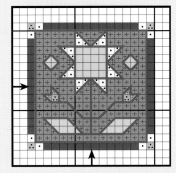

Stitch Count: 16 x 15

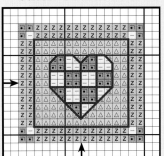

DMC Floss

	X st	BS		X st	BS	FK		X st	BS	FK
White	·		553				3364	·		
Ecru	−		3608				3363			
3823	⊠		3740		⌐		924			⌐
744			341	+			3827	z		
743	◯		775	△			435			⌐
742		⌐	519				415			
976		⌐	3807				318	w		
3713			3811				844			⌐ ●
760	∴		807				3024			
352			806	✳	⌐	●	647	N		
210			772				3021			⌐ ●

Stitch Count: 24 x 55

Stitch Count: 46 x 40

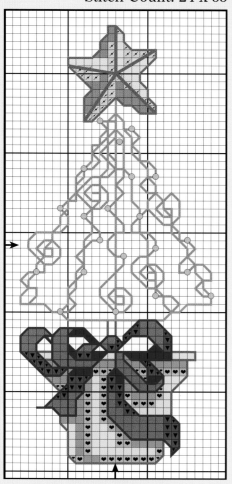

Stitch Count: 23 x 57

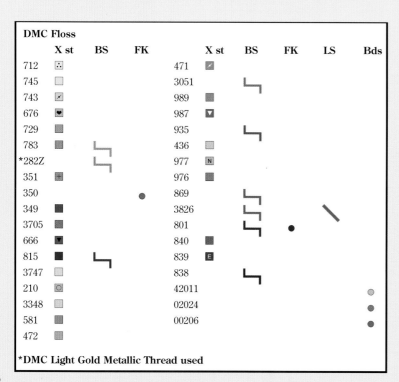

DMC Floss

	X st	BS	FK		X st	BS	FK	LS	Bds
712	⋰			471	◪				
745	▫			3051		⌐			
743	◹			989	▦				
676	♥			987	▼				
729	▦			935		⌐			
783	▦	⌐		436	▫				
*282Z		⌐		977	N				
351	+			976	▦				
350			●	869		⌐			
349	▦			3826		⌐			
3705	▦			801		⌐			
666	▼			840	▦				
815	■	⌐		839	E				
3747	▫			838		⌐			
210	◉			42011					●
3348	▫			02024					●
581	▦			00206					●
472	▦								

*DMC Light Gold Metallic Thread used

Stitch Count: 19 x 31

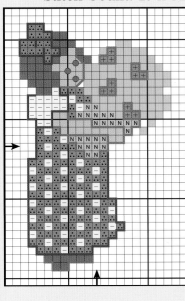

Stitch Count: 14 x 35

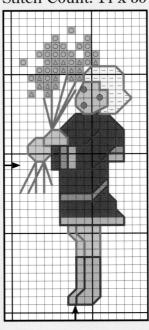

Stitch Count: 28 x 36

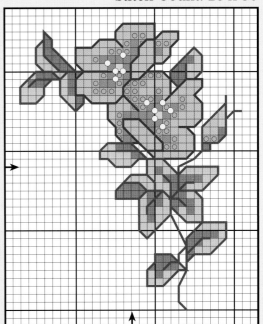

Stitch Count: 35 x 5

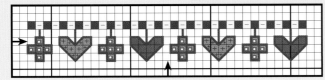

Stitch Count: 20 x 19

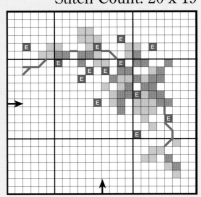

Stitch Count: 40 x 51

Earth laughs in flowers.

DMC Floss							
	X st	BS	FK		X st	BS	FK
Ecru	–		○	3807			
744				791		⌐	●
945				3819			
353				3348			
352	○			3347			
351				3346		⌐	
3712	+			3345		⌐	
815		⌐		472	△	⌐	
3687	E			3051		⌐	
3608				581			
3803		⌐		436	N		
340	⊡			3782			
809	⠂⠂			611		⌐	●
794				3021		⌐	

Stitch Count: 60 x 11

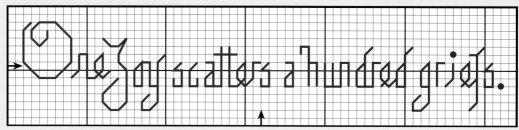

Stitch Count: 34 x 47

Stitch Count: 34 x 21

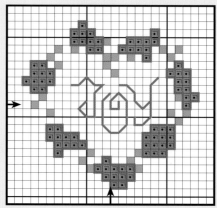

Stitch Count: 22 x 21

Stitch Count: 24 x 31

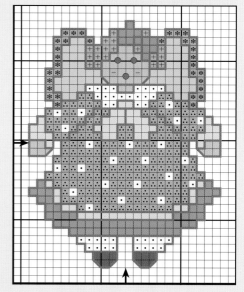

DMC Floss

	X st	BS	FK		X st	BS	FK	Bds
White	·			518			└	
676	+			793				
3045		└		472				
945				471	⊡			
758	−			3051		└		
963				3346				
351				543			○	
210	⫶			437				
554				611		└	●	
553	E			842	N			
327				841				
550		└	●	840				
747				838	■	└	●	
519	✳			00553				○

62

Stitch Count: 19 x 16

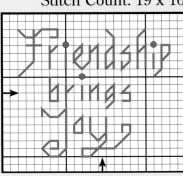

Stitch Count: 13 x 18

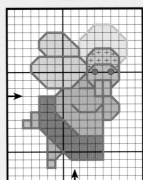

Stitch Count: 15 x 18

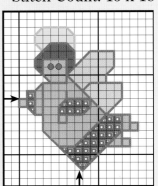

Stitch Count: 32 x 10

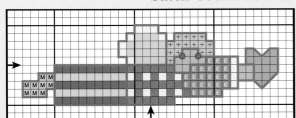

Stitch Count: 33 x 11

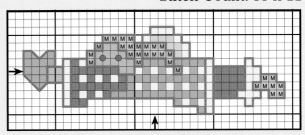

Stitch Count: 34 x 60

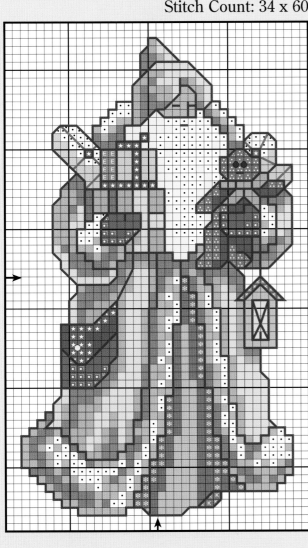

Stitch Count: 28 x 24

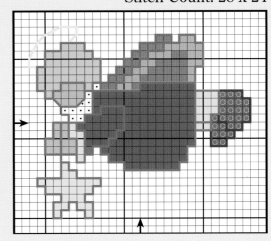

DMC Floss

	X st	BS		X st	BS	FK
White	·		368			
745			3816			
445		⌐	3348			
3822	+		471			
3821		⌐	3012	※		
783			822			○
950			436	M		
3706			976	⚬		
3607			3826		⌐	●
718	✱	⌐	611	◎	⌐	●
341	E		3024			
340			3023			
3746	⊡		3790	K		
775			3031		⌐	●

Stitch Count: 42 x 37

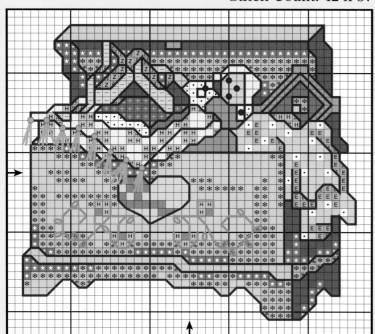

Stitch Count: 20 x 22

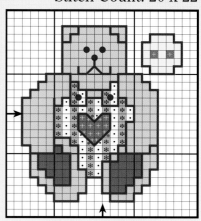

Stitch Count: 23 x 22

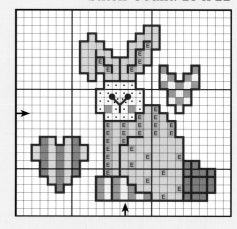

Stitch Count: 26 x 4

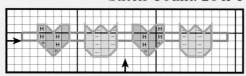

Stitch Count: 50 x 45

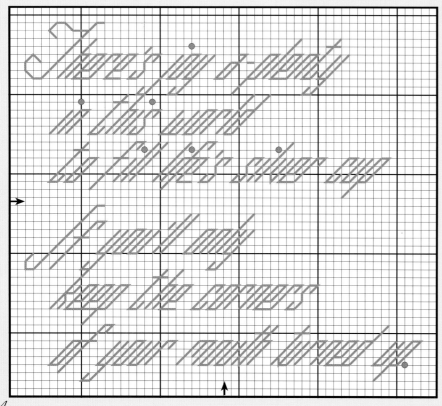

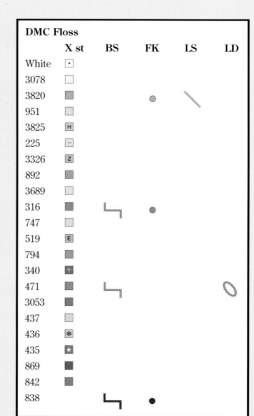

DMC Floss	X st	BS	FK	LS	LD
White	·				
3078					
3820			●	/	
951					
3825	H				
225	−				
3326	Z				
892					
3689					
316		⌐	●		
747					
519	E				
794					
340	+				
471		⌐			O
3053					
437					
436	✳				
435	✶				
869					
842					
838		⌐	●		

Stitch Count: 81 x 20

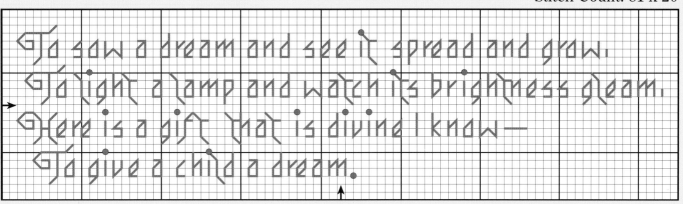

To sow a dream and see it spread and grow.
To light a lamp and watch its brightness gleam.
Here is a gift that is divine I know—
To give a child a dream.

Stitch Count: 62 x 45

DMC Floss						
	X st	**FK**		**X st**	**BS**	**FK**
White	·		471			
727	○		503			
676			502	⊞		
3820		●	3815		⌐	●
945			3768			
3733			437			
223	⊞		436	✳		
3727			356			
316			680			
3761			612			
3755	N		3790	E		
334			3781		⌐	

Stitch Count: 21 x 18

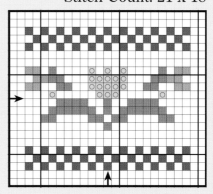

Stitch Count: 33 x 42

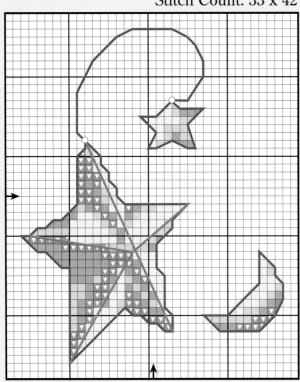

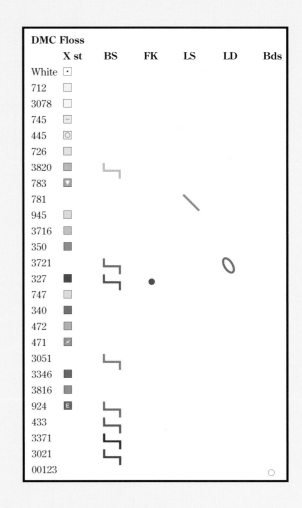

DMC Floss						
	X st	BS	FK	LS	LD	Bds
White	·					
712						
3078						
745	−					
445	◎					
726						
3820		⌐				
783	▽			/		
781						
945						
3716						
350					○	
3721						
327	■	⌐	•			
747						
340						
472						
471	◪					
3051		⌐				
3346	■					
3816						
924	E	⌐				
433		⌐				
3371		⌐				
3021		⌐				
00123						○

Stitch Count: 9 x 55

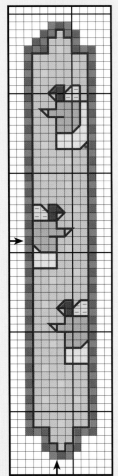

Stitch Count: 24 x 46

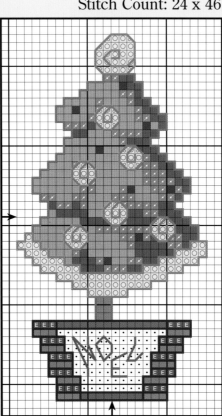

Stitch Count: 25 x 38

Stitch Count: 40 x 26

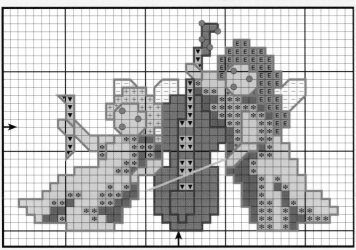

Stitch Count: 27 x 31

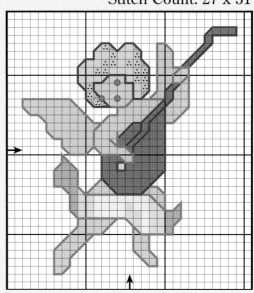

Stitch Count: 37 x 39

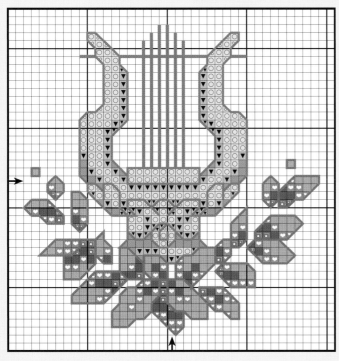

DMC Floss

	X st	BS	LS		X st	BS	FK
Ecru	⊟			3760		⌐	
3823	☐			793	■		
745	◎			3807		⌐	●
727	☐			3750		⌐	●
725	✳			472	▣		
3820	▨			471	♡		
676	▼			3051			
729	▨			3346	▨		
783	▨			437	☐		
3829		⌐		436	⊡		
945	▨			3827	+		
3608	▨			3776	E		
3803		⌐		611	▨	⌐	●
747	☐			801		⌐	
519	✳			3021		⌐	

Stitch Count: 16 x 29

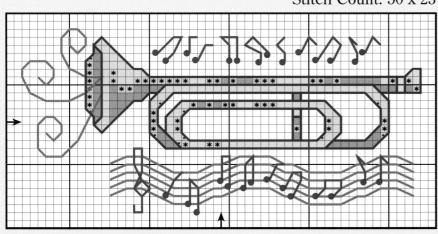

Stitch Count: 50 x 23

Stitch Count: 27 x 27

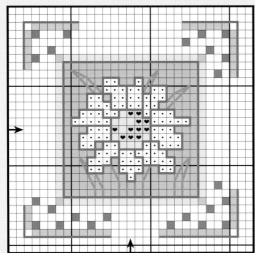

Stitch Count: 23 x 56

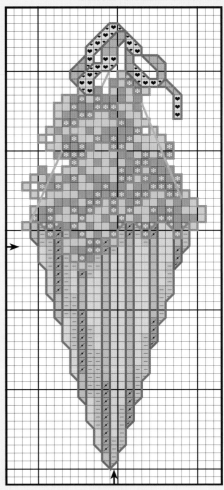

Stitch Count: 34 x 54

Stitch Count: 36 x 9

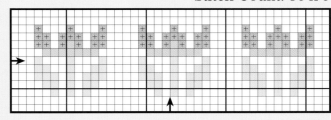

DMC Floss											
	X st	LS	X st	BS	X st	BS	X st	BS	X st	BS	
White	·		776		3803		772		3011		
445			760	+	902		3348	○	520		
307	♥		352		3740		472		989	★	
3822			351		519		471	▼	987		
3821	=		349		340		3819		869		
3820			3687		3746	A	581				

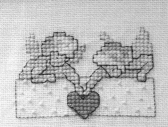

How do you say 'Thank You'
to the angels above
Who've blessed your life
with their magical love?

Stitch Count: 40 x 41

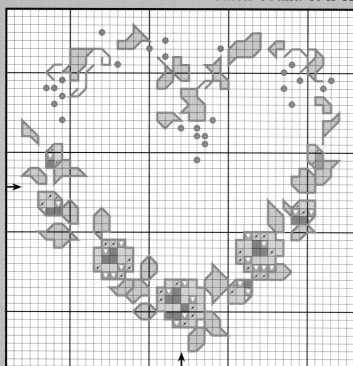

Stitch Count: 15 x 19

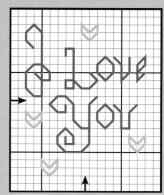

Stitch Count: 30 x 27

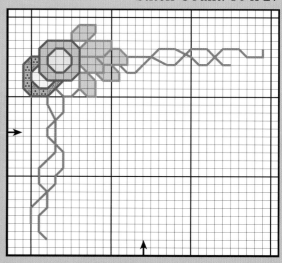

Stitch Count: 29 x 25

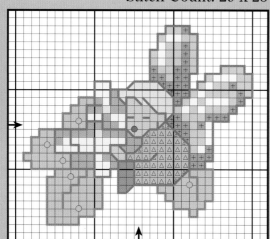

Stitch Count: 23 x 32

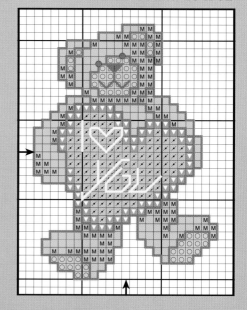

DMC Floss					
	X st	BS		X st	BS	FK
Ecru			3803		
745			3041		
3822			775		
676			3325		
3774			3811		●
353			959		
3712			3348		
3328			3347		●
819			3827		
3716			436		
3806			611		●

Stitch Count: 66 x 12

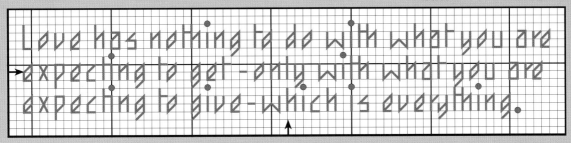

Love has nothing to do with what you are
expecting to get - only with what you are
expecting to give - which is everything.

Stitch Count: 36 x 26

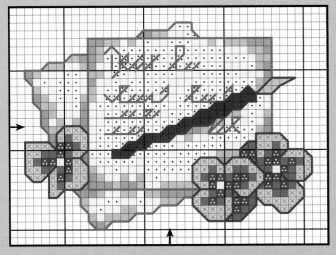

Stitch Count: 34 x 32

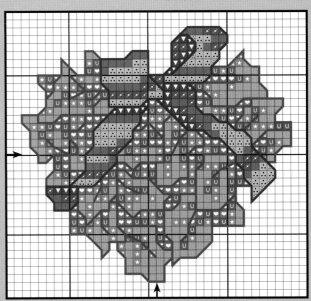

Stitch Count: 24 x 17

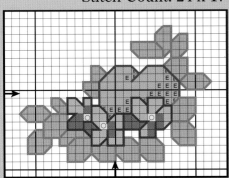

Stitch Count: 26 x 26

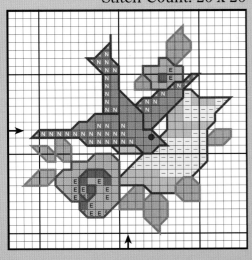

DMC Floss					
	X st	BS		X st	BS	FK
White	·		340	■		
3823	–		813	▨		
3078	▫		322	N		
445	◎		792	▨		
676	▨		791		⌐	
729	▨		3364	▨		
3716	▨		3346	U		
3806	E		472	▨		
3688	▨		471	★		
3687	■		3051	♥		
3803	▨		935		⌐	
3685	▼	⌐	356		⌐	●
902		⌐	610		⌐	
210	▨		3024	▨	⌐	
553	■		844	■	⌐	
3747	⊠		3021		⌐	●

Stitch Count: 15 x 13

Stitch Count: 17 x 7

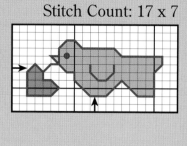

Stitch Count: 13 x 11

Stitch Count: 9 x 10

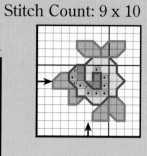

Stitch Count: 42 x 47

Stitch Count: 19 x 19

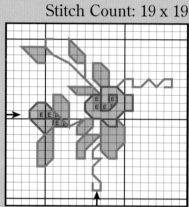

Stitch Count: 12 x 17

Stitch Count: 32 x 25

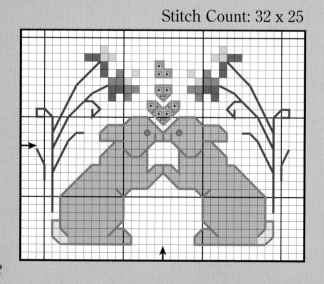

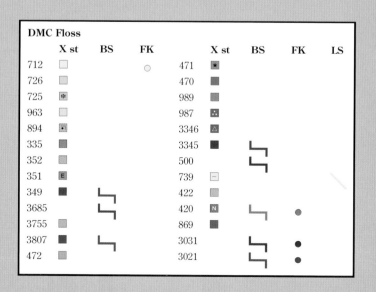

DMC Floss								
	X st	BS	FK		X st	BS	FK	LS
712			○	471	★			
726				470				
725	✳			989				
963				987	▦			
894	▪			3346	△			
335				3345	■			
352				500		⌐		
351	E			739	▬			
349	■			422				
3685		⌐		420	N	⌐		
3755				869				
3807		⌐		3031		⌐	●	
472				3021			●	

Stitch Count: 28 x 8

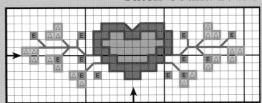

Stitch Count: 44 x 26

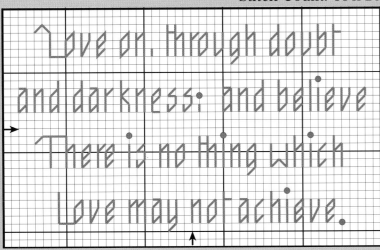

Love on, through doubt and darkness; and believe There is no thing which Love may not achieve.

Stitch Count: 27 x 25

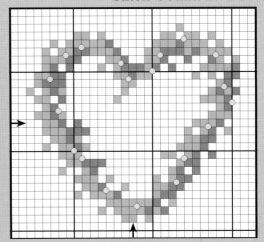

Stitch Count: 21 x 21

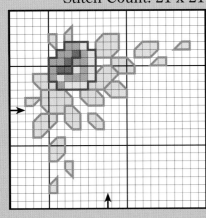

Stitch Count: 44 x 56

DMC Floss					
	X st	BS	FK	LS	Bds
818					
3354					
3731					
3803					
3726			●		
3811	△				
813					
772					
368					
320					
3813					
3816	E				
3815					
739					
437	+				
435					
3827					
3064					
3781					
02018					○

Stitch Count: 19 x 17

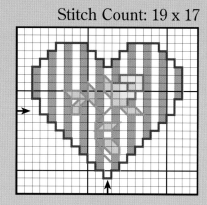

Stitch Count: 19 x 17

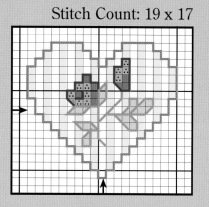

Stitch Count: 19 x 17

Stitch Count: 58 x 10

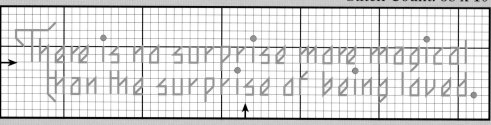

There is no surprise more magical than the surprise of being loved.

DMC Floss

	X st	BS		X st	BS	FK		X st	BS	Bds
White	·		3722	▣			3807		⌐	
445	☐		221		⌐		3348	☐		
948	☐		333		⌐		581		⌐	
3778	▨		341	▨	⌐		368	▨		
3689	+		3041		⌐		3827	☐		
3688	▨		3761	☐			356	▨		
894		⌐	828	△			02019			○
3806	⊡		799		⌐	●	00431			●

Stitch Count: 36 x 36

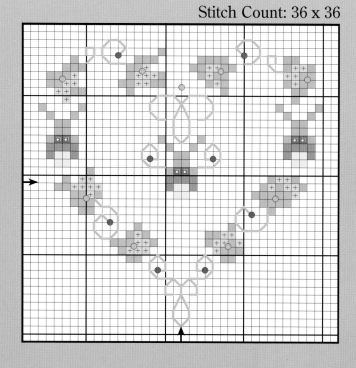

Stitch Count: 30 x 32

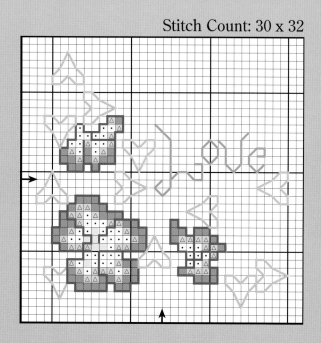

74

Stitch Count: 28 x 16

Stitch Count: 18 x 14

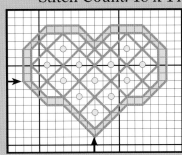

Stitch Count: 19 x 25

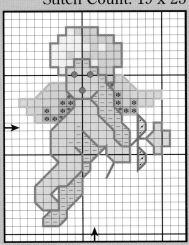

Stitch Count: 46 x 43

How do you say 'Thank You'
to the angels above
Who've blessed your life
with their magical love?

Stitch Count: 24 x 26

Stitch Count: 20 x 27

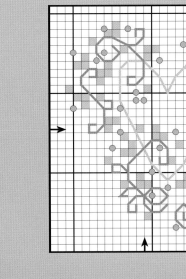

DMC Floss							
	X st	BS	FK	X st	BS	FK	Bds
712	◯			519	✳		
3823	▫			793		⌐	
727	▫			772	◪		
725	+			966	▪		
676	▦			3816		⌐	
3045		⌐		3815		⌐	
3774	▫			3827	▪		
754	–			3776	▪		
760	▨			356		⌐	
3712		⌐		611		⌐	●
3706	△			839		⌐	●
221		⌐	●	02002				○
3747	▫			00275				●
747	▫						

Stitch Count: 37 x 12

With my whole heart I have sought you.

Stitch Count: 13 x 28

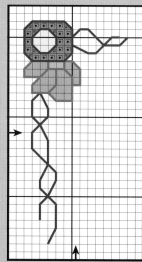

Stitch Count: 18 x 36

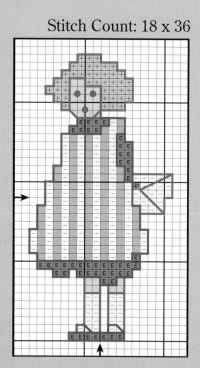

DMC Floss

	X st	BS	FK	LS
White	·			
Ecru	–			
712				
676				
783		⌐	•	
951				
819				
893				
351	·			
350				
817	✳	⌐	•	
902		⌐	•	
3803		⌐		
3685		⌐		
3740		⌐		
341	E			
3752		⌐		
924		⌐	•	
472				
581				
3051		⌐		
738	✓			
437				
436	+			
840		⌐	•	/
3781		⌐		

Stitch Count: 23 x 26

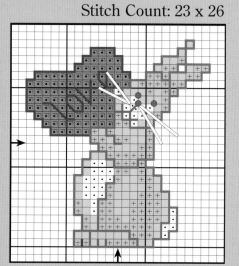

Stitch Count: 43 x 38

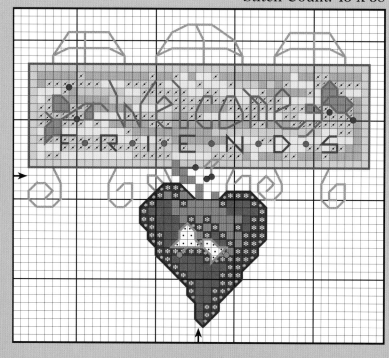

Stitch Count: 16 x 35

Stitch Count: 12 x 18

Stitch Count: 29 x 27

Stitch Count: 37 x 23

There is a silence
born of love,
which expresses
everything.

Stitch Count: 37 x 53

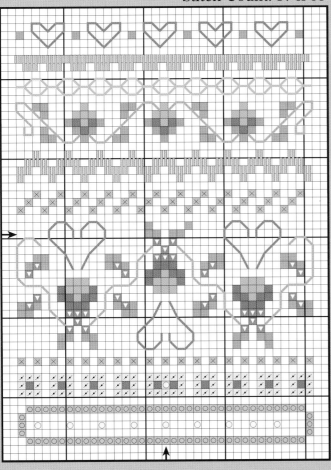

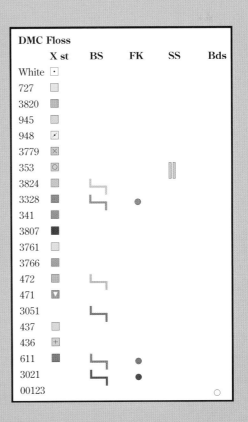

DMC Floss					
	X st	BS	FK	SS	Bds
White	·				
727					
3820					
945					
948					
3779					
353					
3824					
3328					
341					
3807					
3761					
3766					
472					
471					
3051					
437					
436					
611					
3021					
00123					

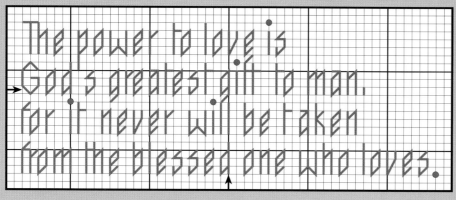

DMC Floss

	X st	BS		X st	BS	FK	Bds
3822			3364	N			
745			472				
754			3346				
3713	✕		3810			●	
3689			3776				
351			356			●	
3806			611				
718			451				
210			00123				○
775			05555				●
966	◉		*MA078807	□			
993			*DC105607				

*Overdyed floss used

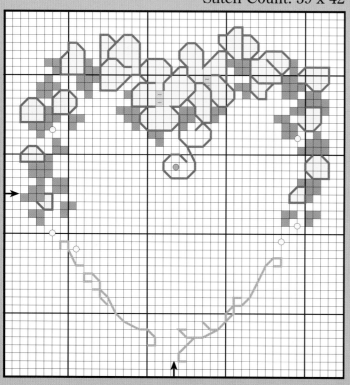

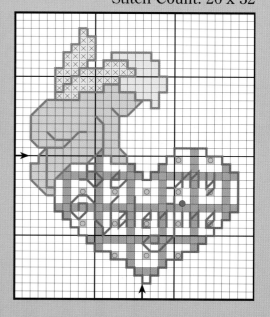

To Rejoice

Code for pages 80-81.

DMC Floss

	X st	BS	FK	LS				Bds
White	·		○		519			
746					747	+		
3078	−				932	★		
445	△		○		794			
307	✳		○		793	⬚		
726					792			●
3820					322			●
3046					564			●
782					3811			●
3774					993			
754	◩				3810			
3806	N		○		924			
957	▪				472			
3712					471	E		
3731					469			
3721					3827			
3803	H				437	○		
211					869			
3740					611			●
340					02019			●

Stitch Count: 18 x 18

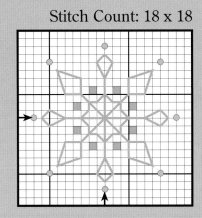

Stitch Count: 11 x 28

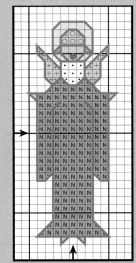

Stitch Count: 16 x 22

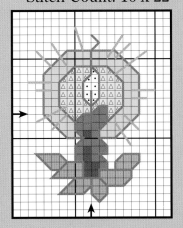

Stitch Count: 23 x 20

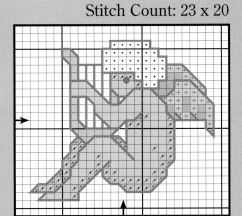

Stitch Count: 37 x 14

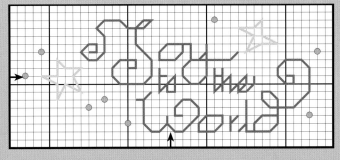

Stitch Count: 18 x 18

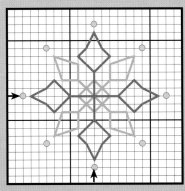

Stitch Count: 51 x 12

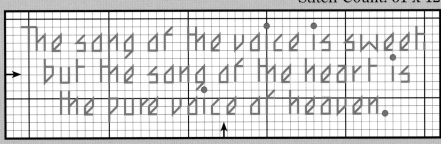

Stitch Count: 41 x 38

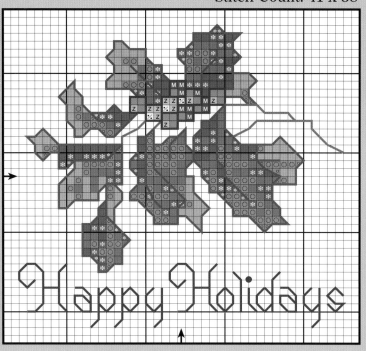

DMC Floss							
	X st	BS	FK		X st	BS	FK
746	▨		○	827	H		
3078	☐			3819	▨		
727	N			3348	☐		
677	☒			3364	U		
676	☐			472	▤		
3046	◈			471	○		
783		⌐		470	◼		
946		⌐		469	✳		
3770	−			936	◼		
951	☐			935			
945	◢			3768		⌐	
776	+			437	☐		
899	☐			436	⠂⠂		
352	Z			420		⌐	
350	◼			869			
347	M			648	N		
3328	△			647	☐		
902		⌐	●	646	▣		
828	☐			844		⌐	●

Stitch Count: 48 x 8

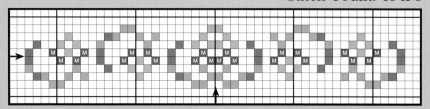

Stitch Count: 18 x 56

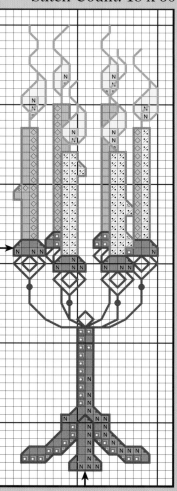

Stitch Count: 51 x 40

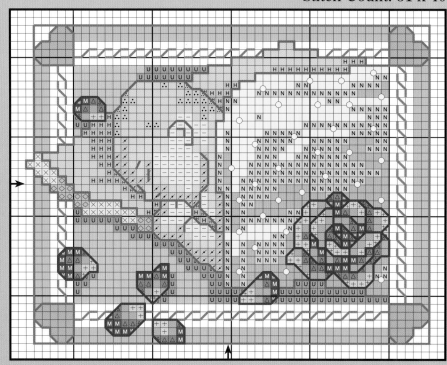

Stitch Count: 54 x 101

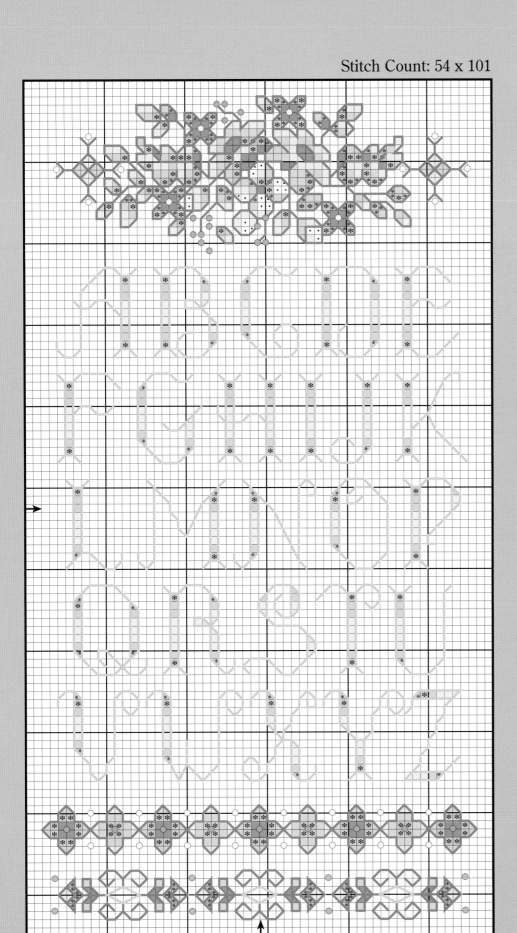

Stitch Count: 12 x 80

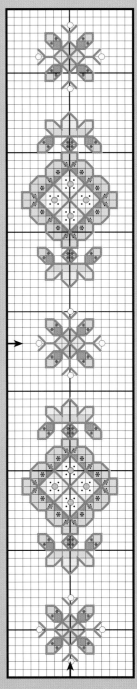

Stitch Count: 14 x 21

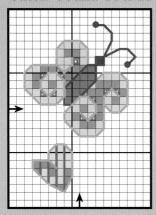

Stitch Count: 40 x 40

Stitch Count: 19 x 15

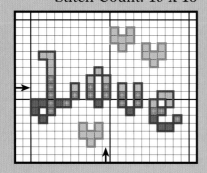

Stitch Count: 10 x 18

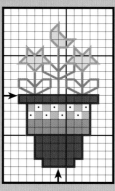

Stitch Count: 34 x 38

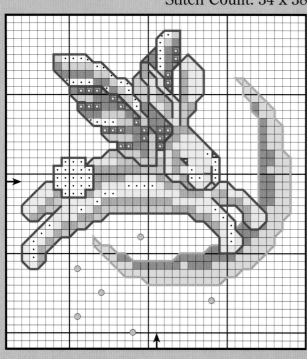

Code for Pages 84-85

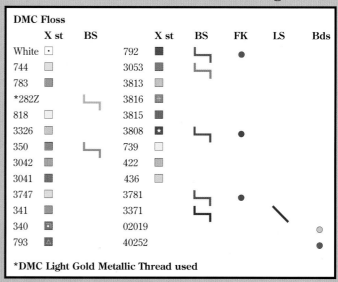

DMC Floss

	X st	BS		X st	BS	FK	LS	Bds
White	⊡		792	■	⌐	●		
744			3053	■	⌐			
783			3813					
*282Z		⌐	3816	✚				
818			3815	■				
3326			3808	★	⌐	●		
350	■		739					
3042			422					
3041	■		436					
3747			3781		⌐	●		
341	■		3371		⌐		—	
340	▨		02019					●
793	▣		40252					●

***DMC Light Gold Metallic Thread used**

84

Stitch Count: 49 x 33

Stitch Count: 18 x 31

Stitch Count: 21 x 8

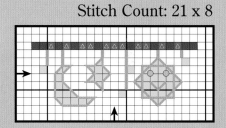

Stitch Count: 18 x 15

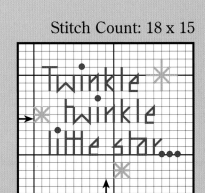

Stitch Count: 43 x 52

Stitch Count: 24 x 27

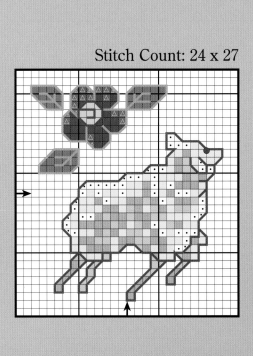

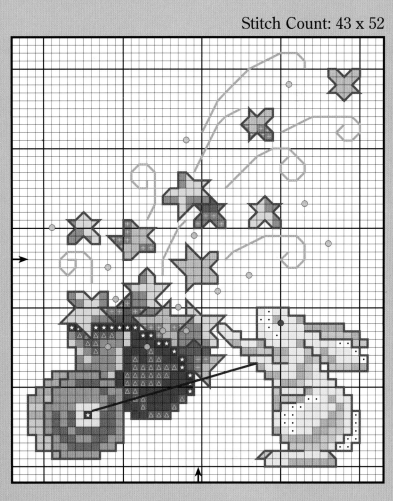

Stitch Count: 129 x 96

Stitch Count: 8 x 74

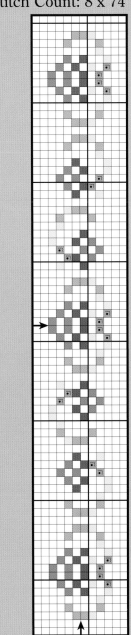

DMC Floss

	X st	BS	FK
818			
3354			●
3733			
3731			
3350			●
3803			

Stitch Count: 49 x 29

Stitch Count: 22 x 8

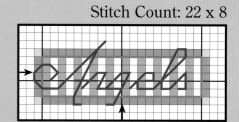

Stitch Count: 62 x 50

DMC Floss													
	X st	BS	FK	LS	X st	BS	X st	BS	X st	BS	FK	LS
712	▢		○		3733 ▨		932 ▨		436 ▬			
3078	▢				3685	⌐	931 ▨	⌐	422 ✚			
744	▨				554 ▨		3348 ▨		356 ▨			
729		⌐			553 ✳		581 ▨		3033 ▨		○	
951	▨				340 ▨		3013 ▨		612 ▨			
352	▨				3746 ▨	⌐	3012 ▨		648 N			
223	✶				3752 ▨		437 ▨		3781	⌐	●	╲

The music of life
is different to each of us...
but, how beautiful the dance!

Continued from page 89.

Stitch Count: 78 x 176

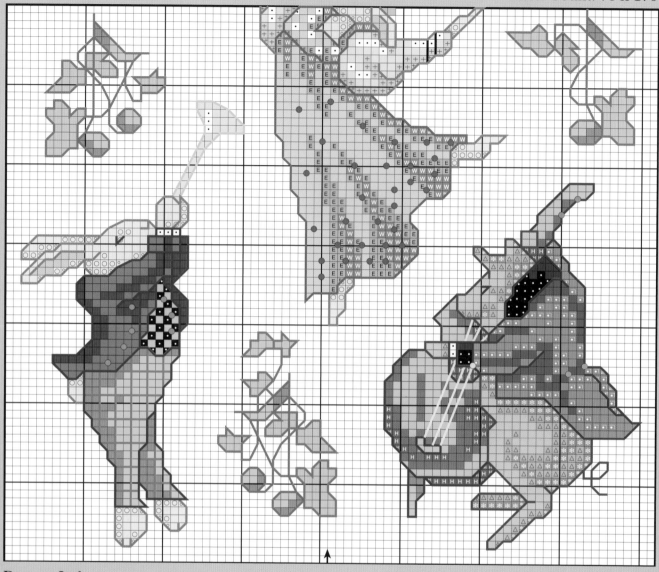

Bottom Left

DMC Floss										
	X st	BS	FK	LS		X st	BS	FK	X st	BS
White	·				347	★			975	H
712			○		817	■			632	
745					3685		⌐		3031	
743	+				747				413	■
725					519	E			310	■
783			●		518	W			*MA023831	
758	△				813				*DC105607	
3778	✳				826	▣				
761		⌐			824	■		⌐		
963					3051		⌐			
3708	▨		○		739	◎				
3706			●		436			⌐		
350		⌐			435	■		⌐		

*Waterlillies floss used

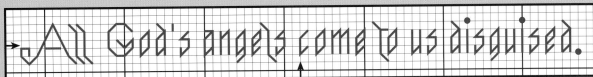

Stitch Count: 38 x 37

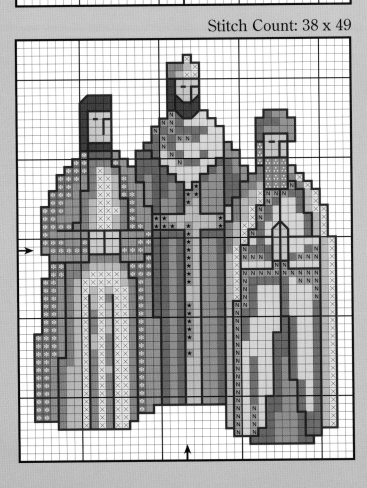

DMC Floss

	X st	BS	FK		X st	BS
White	·			472		
3078				471		
725				3051	E	
677	⊠			3346		
676	+			3813		
729		⌐		502	★	
3046				739		
3045				738	○	
3801				437		
666				420		⌐
815		⌐	●	642		
341				640	✳	
340				647	⋰	
772				451		
522	N			839		
3053				838		⌐

Stitch Count: 22 x 53

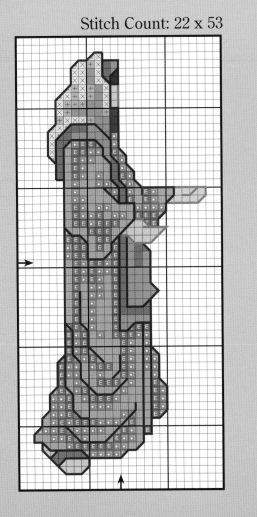

Stitch Count: 38 x 49

To Nurture

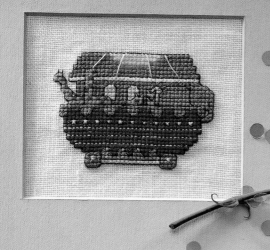

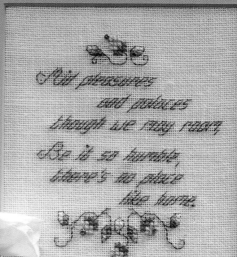

Mid pleasures
and palaces
though we may roam,
Be it so humble,
there's no place
like home.

Make a memory
with your children.
Spend some time
to show you care.
Toys and trinkets
can't replace those
Precious moments
that you share.

Stitch Count: 20 x 10

Stitch Count: 23 x 27

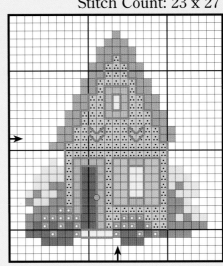

Stitch Count: 36 x 46

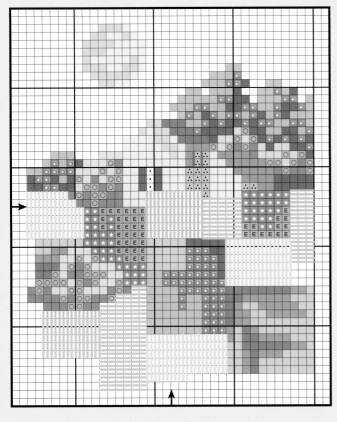

DMC Floss					
	X st		**X st**	**BS**	**FK**	**SS**
White	·	320				
3823		3811				
744		3813				
951		3816				
963		3815			●	
893		3827				
3726		3064			●	
341		356				
747		422				
3325	E	611			●	
813	★	*163				‖‖
772		*178				‖‖
368	◎	*179				‖‖

***Waterlillies floss used**

Stitch Count: 55 x 30

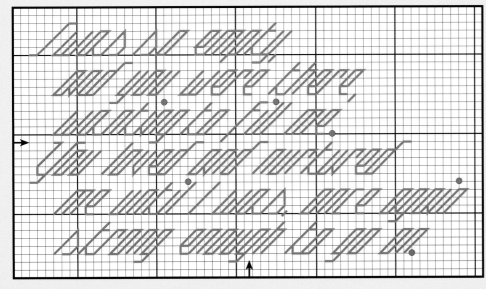

Stitch Count: 15 x 25

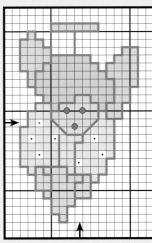

Stitch Count: 43 x 53

Stitch Count: 19 x 12

Stitch Count: 29 x 20

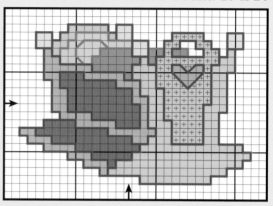

Stitch Count: 16 x 39

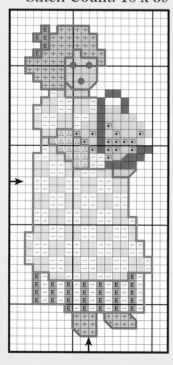

Stitch Count: 25 x 30

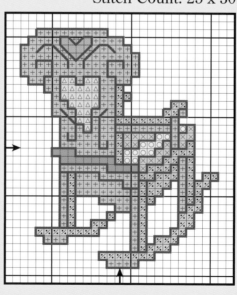

DMC Floss				
	X st	**BS**	**FK**	**Bds**
Ecru	−			
3823	▫			
3078	◉			
445				
951				
3824				
3706	E			
963	△			
3806				
3722	▦			
341				
828				
747	⊠			
3766				
966	⊡			
772				
368	✻			
502		⌐	●	
3827				
437	▨			
436	+			
422				
420		⌐		
611		⌐	●	
840	▦			
839		⌐		
00431				●

Stitch Count: 33 x 47

Stitch Count: 22 x 38

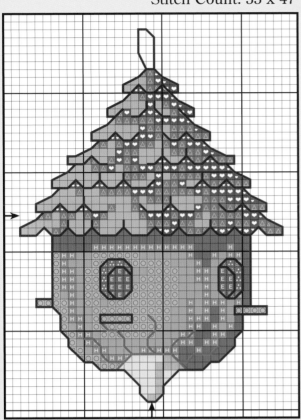

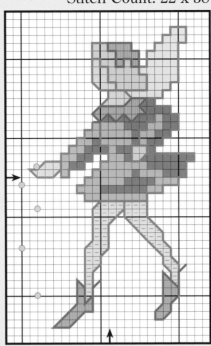

Stitch Count: 44 x 57

DMC Floss				
	X st	BS	FK	Bds
745				
3821				
951				
3354				
3733				
316				
3689				
3806				
718				
3041				
519				
964				
993				
992	H			
807				
3768				
3765				
472				
3346				
3827				
977				
3826				
434	E			
611				
838			●	
02016				●

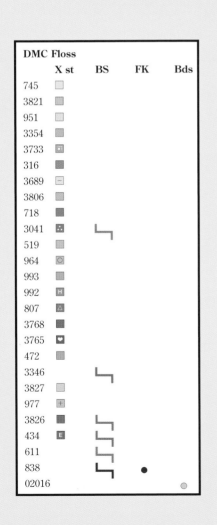

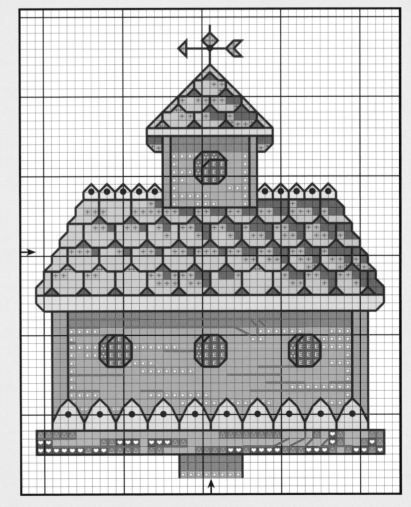

Stitch Count: 22 x 33

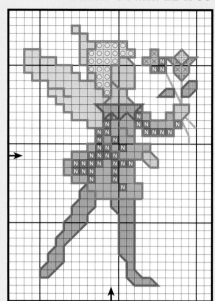

Stitch Count: 44 x 54

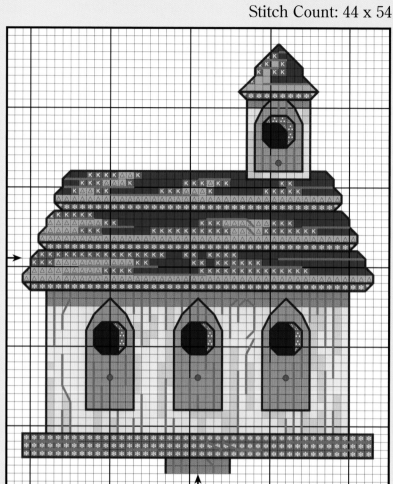

Stitch Count: 32 x 61

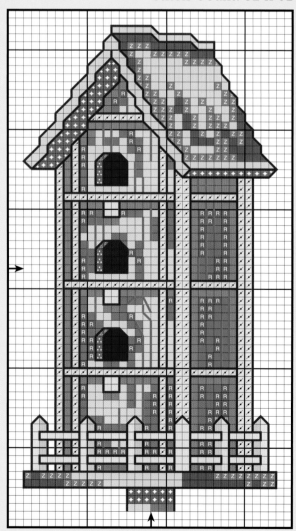

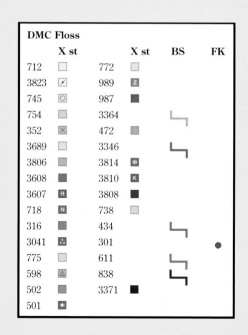

DMC Floss					
	X st		**X st**	**BS**	**FK**
712		772			
3823	◪	989	Z		
745	◉	987			
754		3364		⌐	
352	✕	472	▦		
3689		3346		⌐	
3806		3814	✳		
3608		3810	K		
3607	R	3808			
718	N	738			
316		434		⌐	
3041	❈	301			●
775		611		⌐	
598	△	838		⌐	
502	▥	3371	■		
501	✦				

Stitch Count: 56 x 16

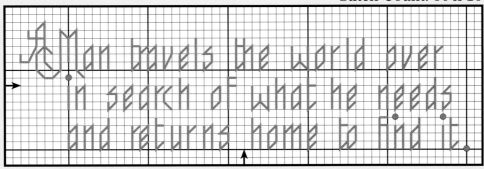

Stitch Count: 36 x 49

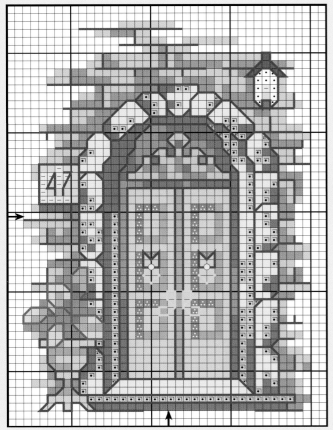

DMC Floss							
	X st	BS	FK		X st	BS	FK
White	·			320			
3823	–			3364			
727	+			472	◎		
744		⌐		3051		⌐	
945				966			
352				3816			
223	✶	⌐		3815		⌐	
3722		⌐	●	739			○
3726				437	·		
3740		⌐		436	E		
341				3827			
828				3064			
3325				435			
813	⊡			611		⌐	●
772				839			
368				3781		⌐	

Stitch Count: 22 x 25

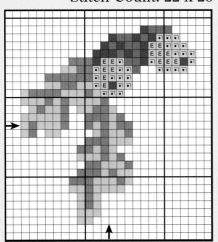

Stitch Count: 32 x 34

97

Stitch Count: 20 x 15

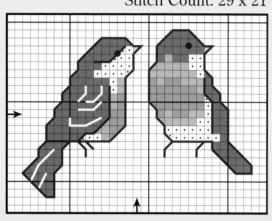

Stitch Count: 27 x 9

Stitch Count: 18 x 9

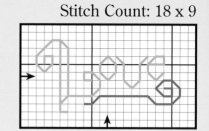

Stitch Count: 29 x 21

Stitch Count: 26 x 29

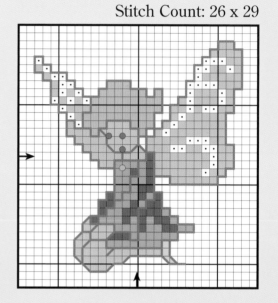

Stitch Count: 19 x 13

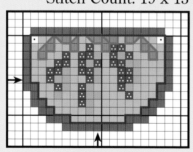

Stitch Count: 24 x 16

O Robin, sing!
for the secret
of eternity
is in song.

Stitch Count: 57 x 26

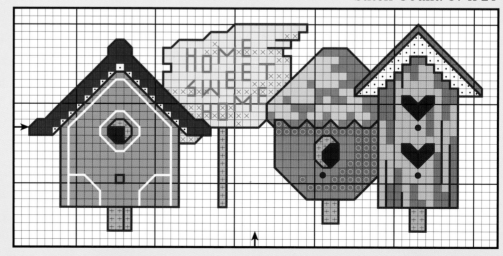

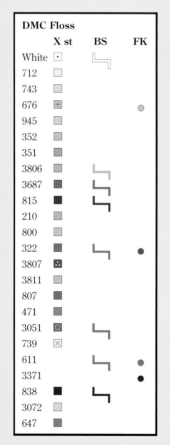

DMC Floss			
	X st	BS	FK
White	·		
712			
743			
676	+		●
945			
352			
351			
3806			
3687			
815			
210			
800			
322			●
3807			
3811			
807			
471			
3051	◎		
739	×		
611			●
3371			●
838			
3072			
647			

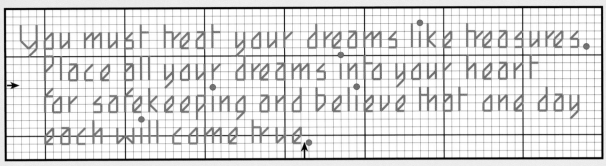

Stitch Count: 41 x 29

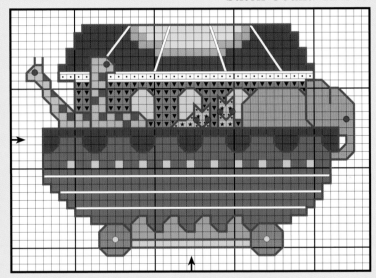

DMC Floss	X st	BS	FK	LS
White	·			
744			●	
3340				
3042				
718		⌐	●	
747				
334	▼			
825				
563				
3819				
472				
471	◪			
470	▼			
469		⌐		
936		⌐		
520		⌐		
3809		⌐		
3827	★			
977				
3828				
869		⌐		
301				
839		⌐	●	

Stitch Count: 48 x 34

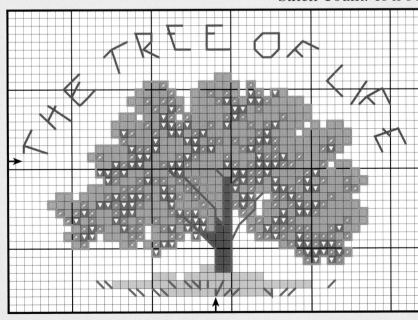

Stitch Count: 54 x 7

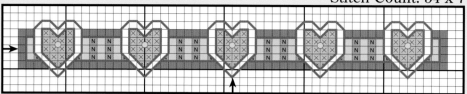

Stitch Count: 54 x 10

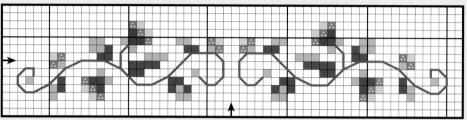

Stitch Count: 33 x 69

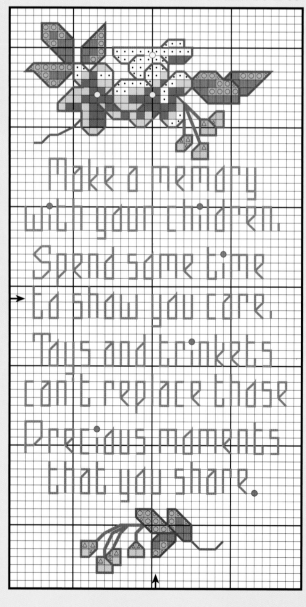

DMC Floss							
	X st	BS	FK		X st	BS	FK	LS
White	·			340	◼		
Ecru	–		○	3761			○
745				828			
761				966	⊠		
760	▲			368			
3328				367		⌐	
347		⌐	●	993	N	⌐	
223		⌐	●	3813	⊙		
211				3816			
209	⊠			3815		⌐	
208	◼			924		⌐	
3747				420			
3740		⌐		869		⌐	╱

Stitch Count: 32 x 32

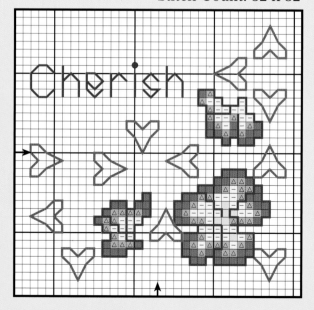

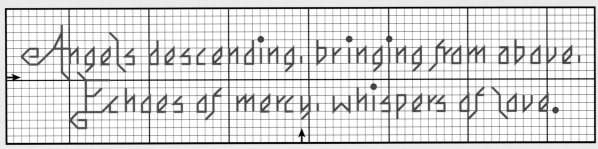

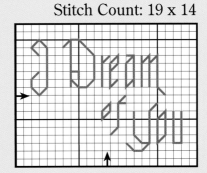

DMC Floss

	X st		X st	BS	FK		X st	BS
White	·	224				501		
3823	▼	223				500		
3822		3722				437		
951		718				436	*	
945	A	3807			●	422	*	
3773		503	N			869		
225								

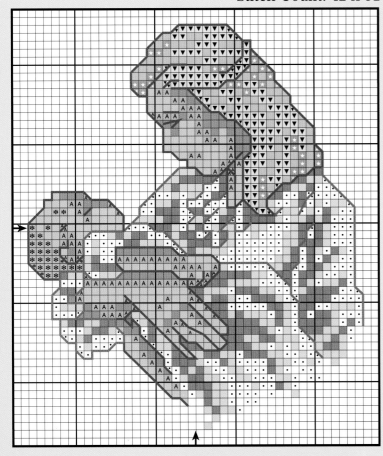

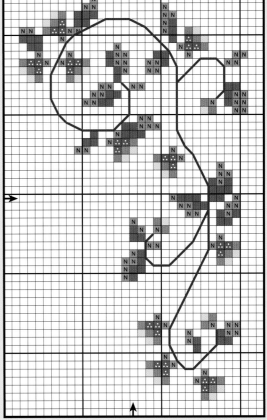

Come read to me some poem
Some simple and heartfelt lay
That shall soothe this restless feeling
And banish the thoughts of day.

Stitch Count: 29 x 50

DMC Floss

	X st	BS	FK		X st	BS	FK
White	·			3747			
3823	▼			340			
3822			○	598	♥		
3821		⌐	○	597			●
951				3811			
945	A			3813	H		
3773				3816			
761				320			
760	✎			924		⌐	
225	⊠			437			
224	✕			436	✳		
223		⌐	●	422	★		
3716				3828			
335				420	⊞		
210				869		⌐	
553							

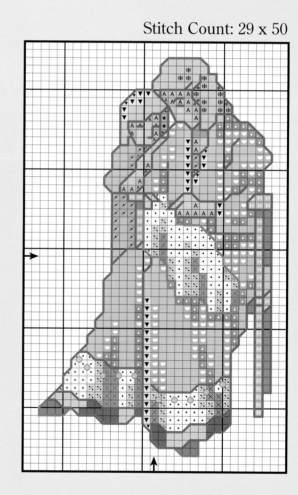

Stitch Count: 31 x 32

Stitch Count: 24 x 19

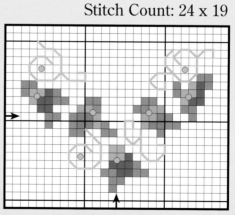

Stitch Count: 33 x 55

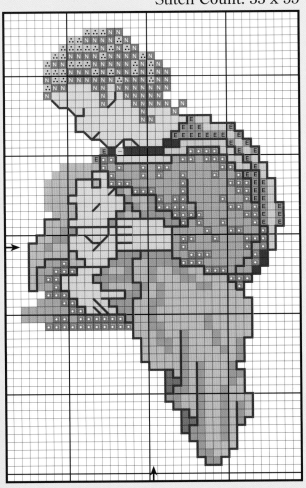

Stitch Count: 35 x 39

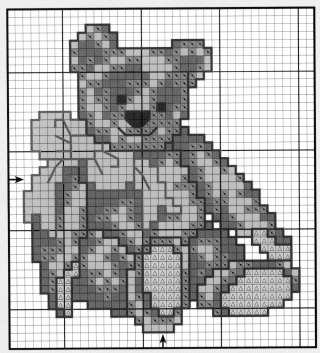

Stitch Count: 45 x 38

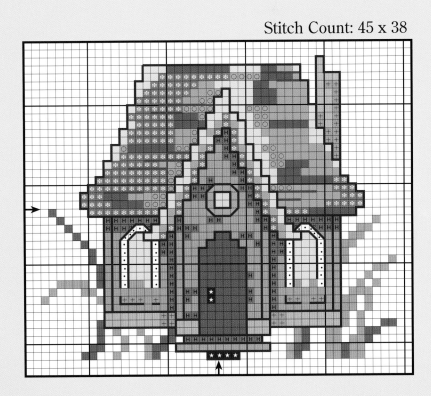

DMC Floss

	X st	BS		X st	BS
White	·		930	■	
745			3750		⌐
744	−		3364	▦	
676			3362	■	
729			504		
3829			502	E	
754			500	■	
3688			436		
3803		⌐	435	N	
3727			3827	△	
3726	◪		977		
3743			976		
3042	+		3826	■	
3740			422		
3756			613		
3752	○		611	H	
932			801	■	
931	✳		838	★	

To Share

Add some tender loving care to your GARDEN

LOVE grows HERE

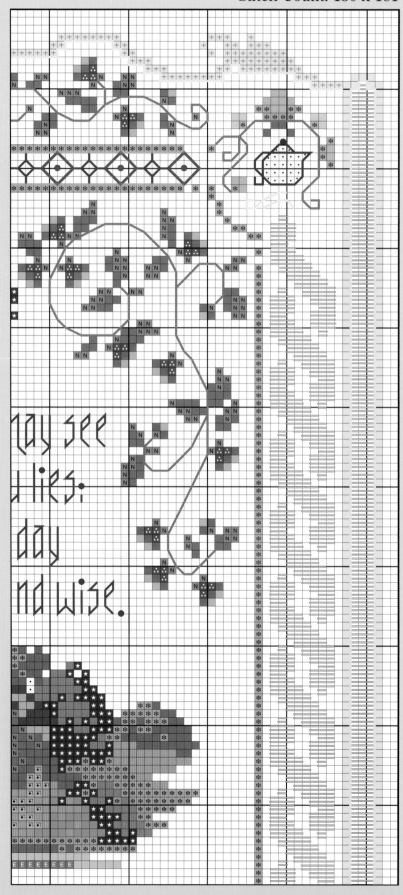

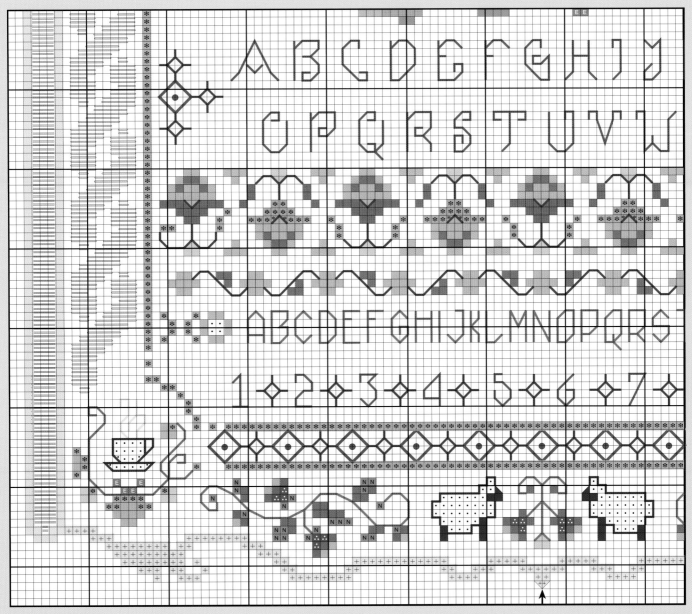

Bottom Left

Code for Pages 105-108

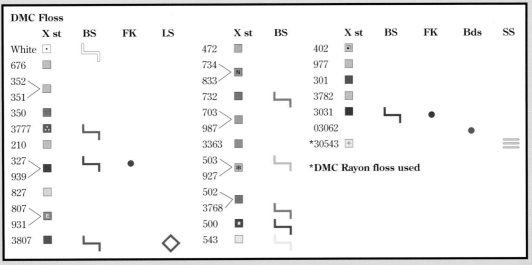

DMC Floss											
	X st	BS	FK	LS	X st	BS	X st	BS	FK	Bds	SS
White	·	⌐			472		402				
676					734	N	977				
352					833		301				
351					732	⌐	3782	⌐			
350					703		3031	⌐	●		
3777		⌐			987		03062			●	
210					3363		*30543	⊞			≡
327		⌐	●		503		*DMC Rayon floss used				
939					927	⌐					
827					502						
807	E				3768	⌐					
931					500	✦	⌐				
3807		⌐		◇	543		⌐				

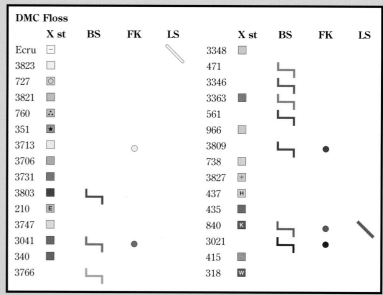

Stitch Count: 14 x 24

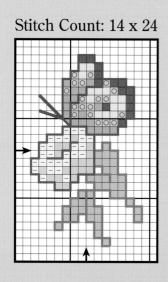

Code for graph at left and page 109.

DMC Floss									
	X st	BS	FK	LS		X st	BS	FK	LS
Ecru	⊟			╱	3348	▨			
3823	▢				471		⌐		
727	◎				3346		⌐		
3821	▨				3363	▨	⌐		
760	⦂				561		⌐		
351	★				966	▨			
3713	▢		◯		3809		⌐	●	
3706	▨				738	▨			
3731	▨				3827	⊞			
3803	■	⌐			437	⊞			
210	Ⓔ				435	▨			
3747	▢				840	K	⌐	⦂	╲
3041	▨	⌐	●		3021		⌐	●	
340	▨				415	▨			
3766		⌐			318	W			

Stitch Count: 19 x 16

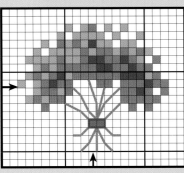

Stitch Count: 10 x 8

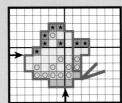

Stitch Count: 13 x 14

Stitch Count: 53 x 10

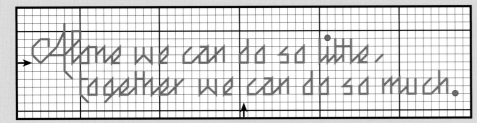

Stitch Count: 18 x 18

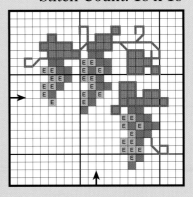

Stitch Count: 52 x 29

Stitch Count: 8 x 20

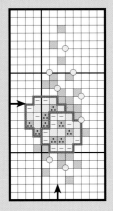

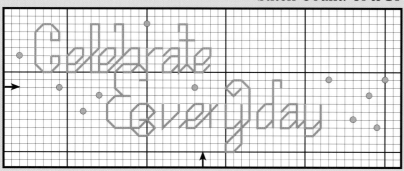

Stitch Count: 46 x 16

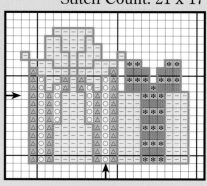

Stitch Count: 21 x 17

DMC Floss

	X st	BS	FK		X st	BS		X st	BS	Bds
White	·		○	3716	N		334			
712	−		○	351			311			
746	⊠			3328			3348			
745				210	⁂		3012	★		
3078	◎			3041			471			
445				3756			3051			
725				827	▼		936			
3045				964	✳		3827	+		
783				3766			869			
945				3755	◪		844	■		
760				518			02019			●
894	△									

Stitch Count: 23 x 35

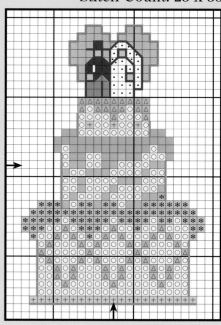

Stitch Count: 43 x 49

Stitch Count: 22 x 35

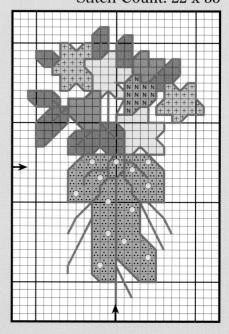

Stitch Count: 25 x 52

Stitch Count: 13 x 21

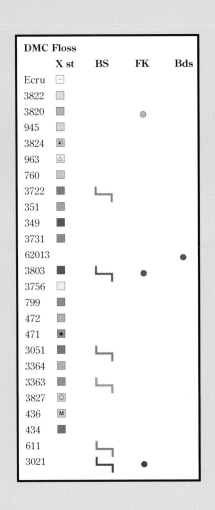

Stitch Count: 17 x 16

DMC Floss				
	X st	**BS**	**FK**	**Bds**
Ecru	⊟			
3822	▨			
3820	▨		●	
945	▨			
3824	▨			
963	△			
760	▨			
3722	▨	⌐		
351	▨			
349	▨			
3731	▨			
62013				●
3803	▨	⌐	●	
3756	▨			
799	▨			
472	▨			
471	★			
3051	▨	⌐		
3364	▨			
3363	▨	⌐		
3827	◎			
436	M			
434	▨			
611		⌐		
3021		⌐	●	

Stitch Count: 26 x 26

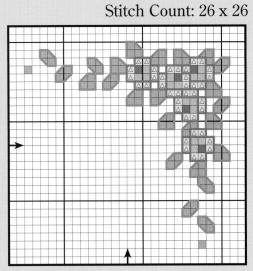

Stitch Count: 40 x 20

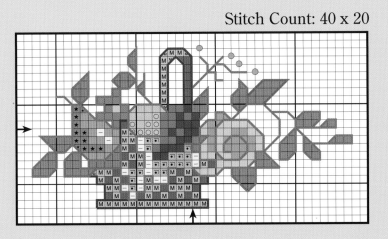

Stitch Count: 67 x 11

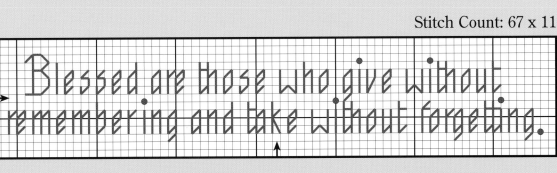

Stitch Count: 38 x 35

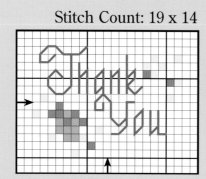

Stitch Count: 19 x 14

Stitch Count: 79 x 40

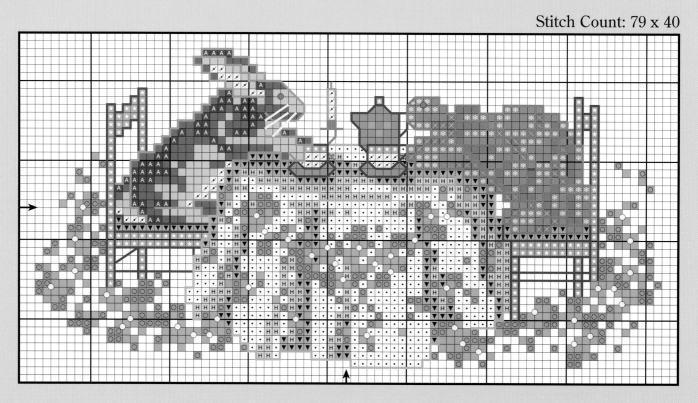

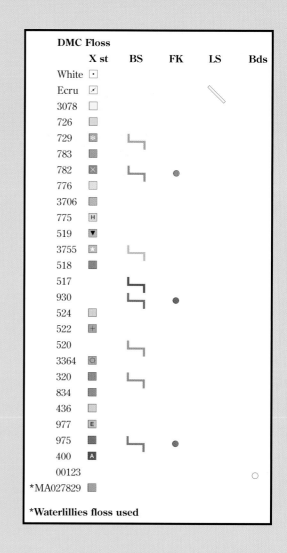

DMC Floss					
	X st	**BS**	**FK**	**LS**	**Bds**
White	·				
Ecru	⊠				
3078	☐				
726	☐				
729	✳	⌐			
783	☐				
782	✕	⌐	●		
776	☐				
3706	☐				
775	H				
519	▼				
3755	✶	⌐			
518	☐				
517		⌐			
930		⌐	●		
524	☐				
522	⊞				
520		⌐			
3364	◎				
320	☐	⌐			
834	☐				
436	☐				
977	E				
975	☐	⌐	●		
400	A				
00123					○
*MA027829	☐				

*Waterlillies floss used

112

Stitch Count: 35 x 34

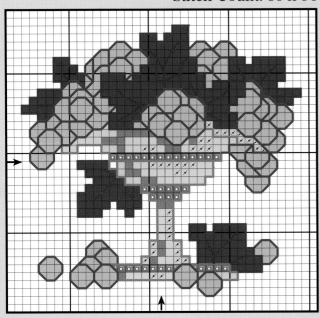

Stitch Count: 21 x 24

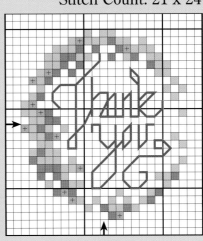

Stitch Count: 74 x 10

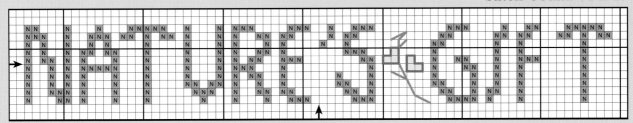

Stitch Count: 34 x 40

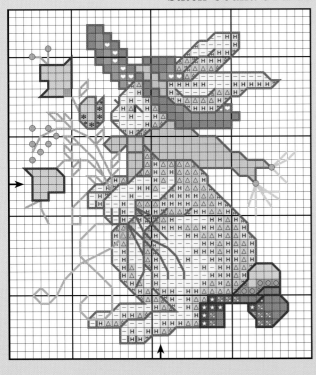

DMC Floss							
	X st	BS	FK		X st	BS	FK
Ecru	⊟			3816	▦		
745	H			319	■		
3822	▣			834	▦		
3821	✳			738	✎		
729	▦			437	▢		
783	♡			3827	△		
780		⌐		976	▦		
3713	▢			975	▨		
3354	⊞			400	★		
3687		⌐		435	▦		
747	▢			434	▣		
3766	◎	⌐	●	3829		⌐	
3807		⌐		801		⌐	
939		⌐		*MA053901	▣		
471		⌐		*MA0061030	▦		
890		⌐		*MA027829	▣		
966	▣			*DC105607	N	⌐	●
*Waterlillies floss used							

Stitch Count: 46 x 26

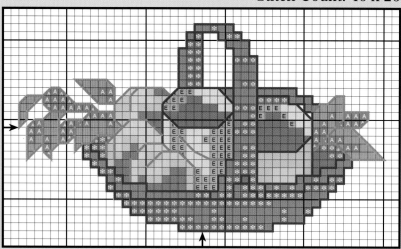

Stitch Count: 50 x 61

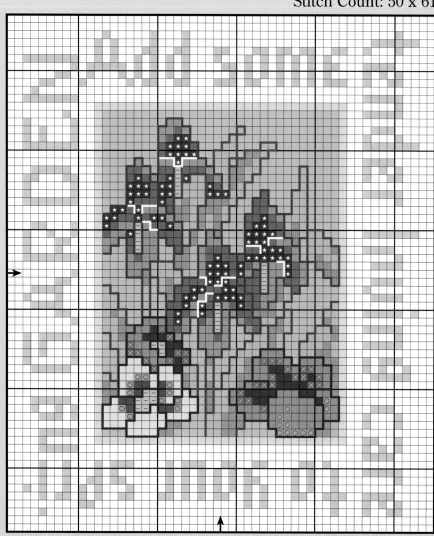

Stitch Count: 23 x 31

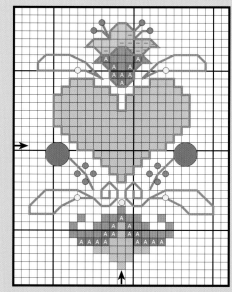

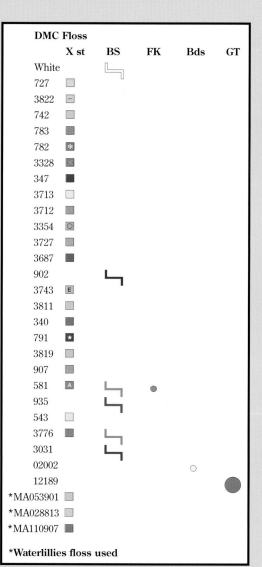

DMC Floss

	X st	BS	FK	Bds	GT
White					
727					
3822					
742					
783					
782					
3328					
347					
3713					
3712					
3354					
3727					
3687					
902					
3743					
3811					
340					
791					
3819					
907					
581					
935					
543					
3776					
3031					
02002					
12189					
*MA053901					
*MA028813					
*MA110907					

*Waterlillies floss used

Stitch Count: 29 x 29

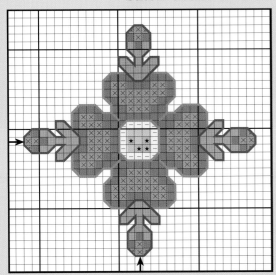

Stitch Count: 29 x 29

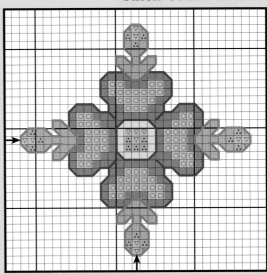

Stitch Count: 50 x 51

DMC Floss		
	X st	BS
Ecru	⊟	
745		
761		
760	★	
3712	⊠	
3328	⊡	
347	■	⌐
778	◎	
316	▦	
315		⌐
3743		
3041		⌐
3753	▽	
932	⊡	
928		
926		⌐
503		
501		⌐
472		
581	✳	⌐
935		⌐

To Sow

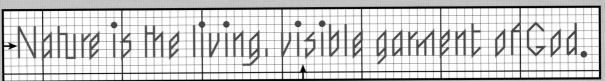

Stitch Count: 39 x 47

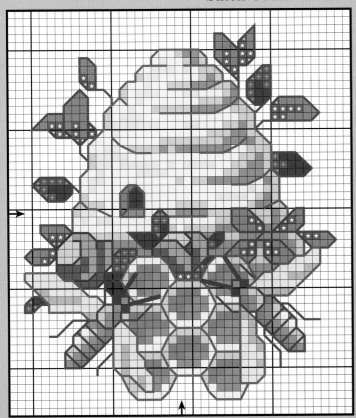

DMC Floss

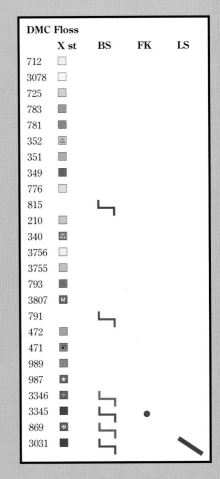

	X st	BS	FK	LS
712				
3078				
725				
783				
781				
352	△			
351				
349				
776				
815		⌐		
210				
340	⊞			
3756				
3755				
793				
3807	M			
791		⌐		
472				
471	▪			
989				
987	★			
3346	+	⌐		
3345		⌐	●	
869	✳	⌐		
3031		⌐		╱

Stitch Count: 77 x 9

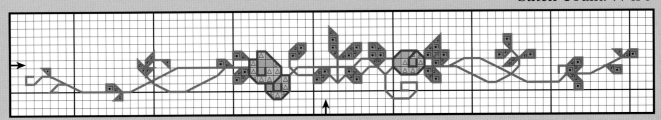

Stitch Count: 25 x 12

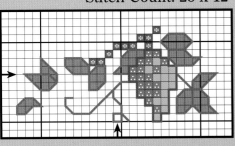

Stitch Count: 5 x 15

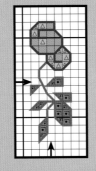

Stitch Count: 24 x 17

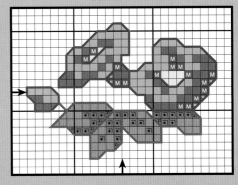

Stitch Count: 11 x 16

Stitch Count: 17 x 18

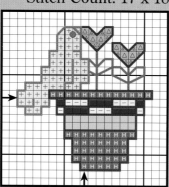

Stitch Count: 33 x 60

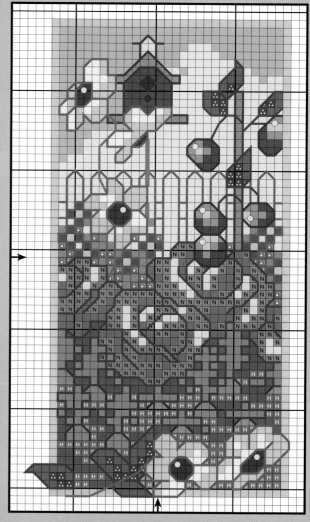

Stitch Count: 30 x 8

Stitch Count: 30 x 18

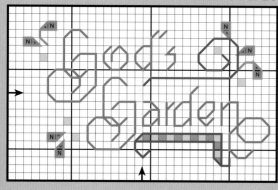

Stitch Count: 15 x 10

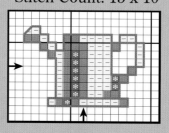

Stitch Count: 13 x 11

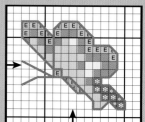

DMC Floss

	X st	BS	FK		X st	BS	FK
Ecru	−			3807	■	⌐	
712	☐		○	472	☐		
3823	+			471	N	⌐	
3078	☐			470	■		
727	☐			989	■		
725	☐			987	▣		
783	☐			3346	■	⌐	
781		⌐		3345	▩	⌐	
776	☐			500	■	⌐	
760	△			436	E		
351	■			420	H		
349	■			869	■	⌐	
221	■	⌐		612	☐		
341	☐			611	✳	⌐	●
3756	☐			3031	■	⌐	●
3755	☐			3021	★	⌐	

Stitch Count: 9 x 16

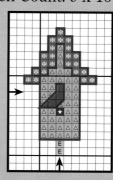

Stitch Count: 16 x 20

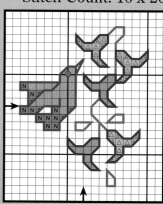

Stitch Count: 60 x 9

Stitch Count: 41 x 51

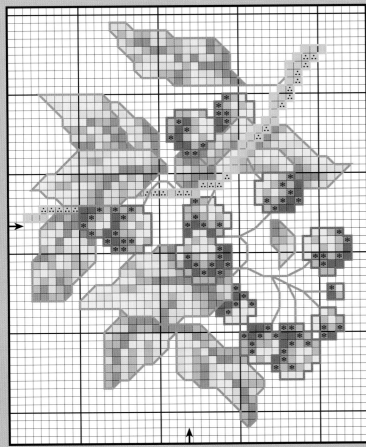

Stitch Count: 14 x 9

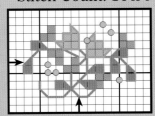

Stitch Count: 27 x 26

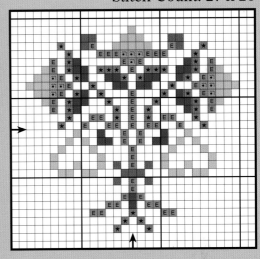

Stitch Count: 35 x 27

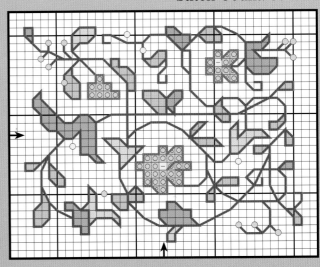

DMC Floss

	X st	BS	FK		X st	BS
3078			○	959		
3823				3348		
3821			●	581	E	
948				471		
3824				561		
3778	✳			772		
3722				368		
776	◎		●	502		
3712	⊡			501	★	
351				500		
3609				738		
3687			●	437	⊡	
3761				436		

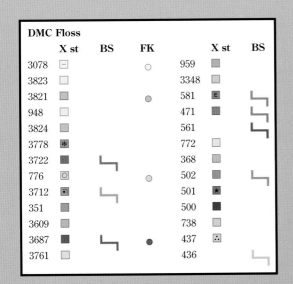

Stitch Count: 24 x 19

Stitch Count: 18 x 18

Stitch Count: 21 x 24

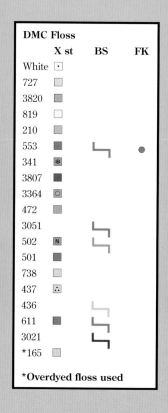

Stitch Count: 44 x 54

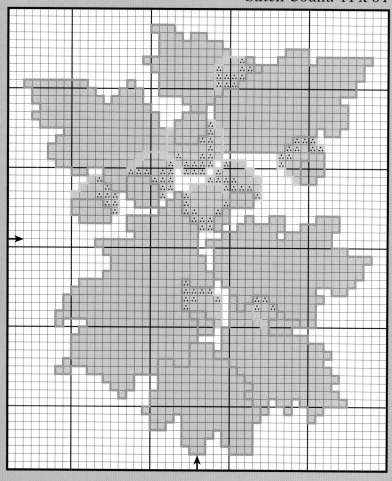

DMC Floss			
	X st	BS	FK
White	·		
727			
3820			
819			
210			
553		⌐	●
341	✳		
3807			
3364	◎		
472			
3051		⌐	
502	N		
501			
738			
437	⦂		
436		⌐	
611			
3021		⌐	
*165			

*Overdyed floss used

Stitch Count: 26 x 26

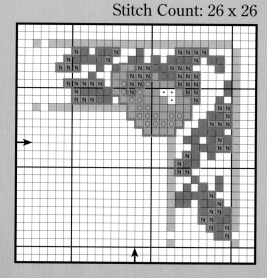

Stitch Count: 46 x 18

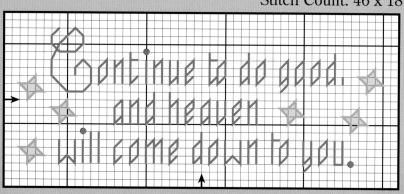

Continue to do good, and heaven will come down to you.

Stitch Count: 65 x 11

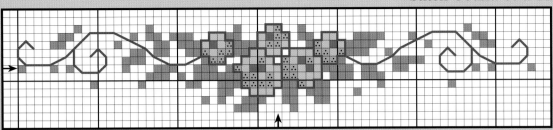

Stitch Count: 38 x 58

Stitch Count: 30 x 29

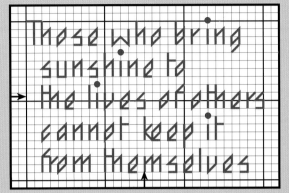

Those who bring
sunshine to
the lives of others
cannot keep it
from themselves

Stitch Count: 23 x 27

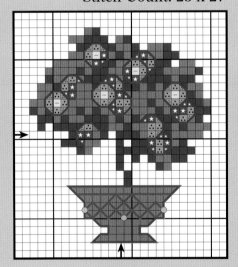

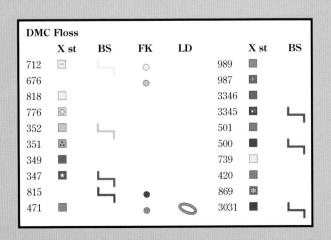

DMC Floss							
	X st	BS	FK	LD		X st	BS
712	–		○		989		
676			○		987	+	
818					3346		
776	○				3345		
352					501		
351					500		
349					739		
347	★				420		
815			●		869	✳	
471			●	⬭	3031		

121

Stitch Count: 12 x 15

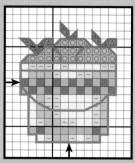

Stitch Count: 23 x 22

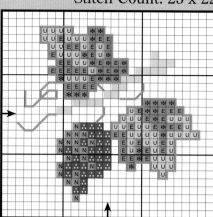

Stitch Count: 16 x 31

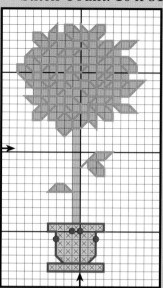

Stitch Count: 26 x 12

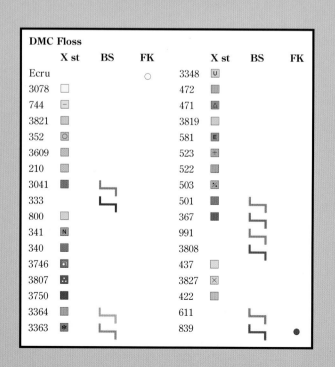

Stitch Count: 29 x 5

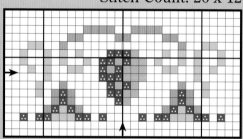

Stitch Count: 40 x 48

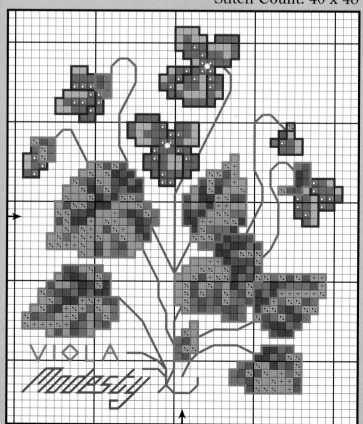

DMC Floss

	X st	BS	FK		X st	BS	FK
Ecru			○	3348	U		
3078	☐			472			
744	−			471	△		
3821				3819			
352	○			581	E		
3609				523	+		
210				522			
3041		⌐		503	▨		
333		⌐		501			
800				367		⌐	
341	N			991		⌐	
340				3808		⌐	
3746	▣			437			
3807	▨			3827	☒		
3750				422			
3364		⌐		611		⌐	
3363	✳	⌐		839		⌐	●

Stitch Count: 49 x 30

Stitch Count: 36 x 31

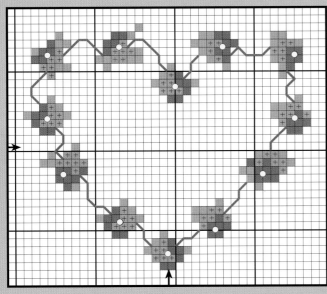

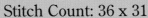

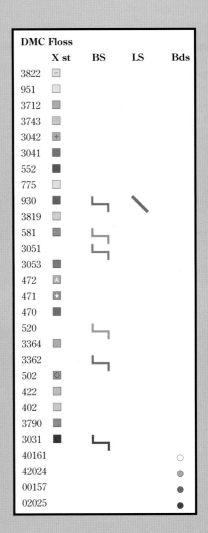

DMC Floss				
	X st	BS	LS	Bds
3822	⊟			
951				
3712				
3743				
3042	+			
3041				
552				
775				
930		⌐	/	
3819				
581		⌐		
3051		⌐		
3053				
472	A			
471	★			
470				
520		⌐		
3364				
3362		⌐		
502	⊙			
422				
402				
3790		⌐		
3031		⌐		
40161				○
42024				●
00157				●
02025				●

Stitch Count: 70 x 21

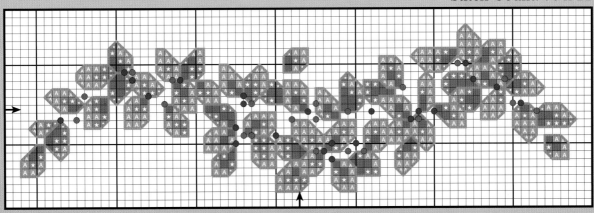

123

Stitch Count: 44 x 24

Stitch Count: 11 x 13

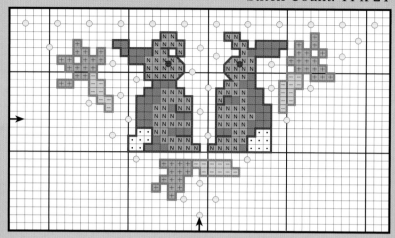

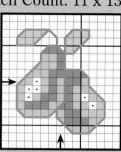

Stitch Count: 22 x 14

Stitch Count: 46 x 20

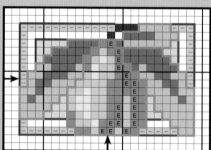

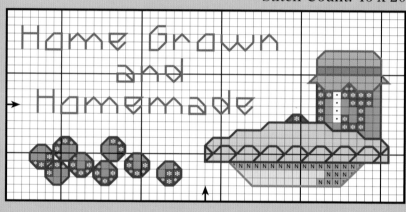

Stitch Count: 38 x 46

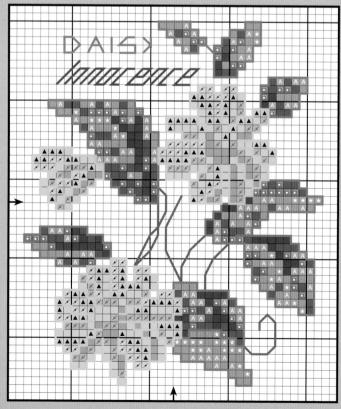

DMC Floss							
	X st	**BS**	**FK**		**X st**	**BS**	**FK**
White	·			523	✽		
712	▫			522	▪		
445			○	3363	E	⌐	
727	◢			367	▪		
444	▫			503	A		
3822	▲			501	▪	⌐	
3821	◢			3817	▫		
3820	▪			3815	▪		
3354	▪			991		⌐	
3731	▪			3808		⌐	
3350		⌐		738	▫		
3761	▫			3827	▭		
794	▪			436	▫		
3807	✽			611		⌐	
311		⌐		801		⌐	
3750	▪			3021	▪	⌐	
3348	▫			762	▫		
472	✚			415	N		
3819	▫			414	▪		
581	▪	⌐		413		⌐	●
3051		⌐					

Stitch Count: 40 x 41

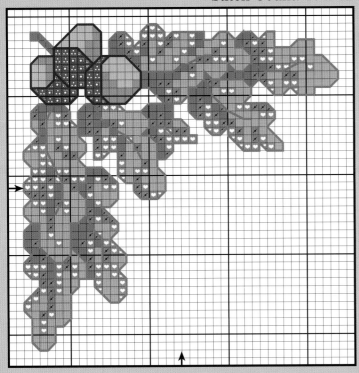

DMC Floss

	X st	BS	FK
822	☐		○
3822	⊟		
676	▦		
729	▦		
783	▦		
472	▦		
471	♡		
3012	▦		
3011	◎		
3347	▨		
3051	▦		
936		⌐	
420	▦		
3826	N		
301	▣		
400	▦		
433	▣		
3031		⌐	●
838		⌐	
3782	▨		
642	✦		
646	▦		
3787	■		

Stitch Count: 65 x 41

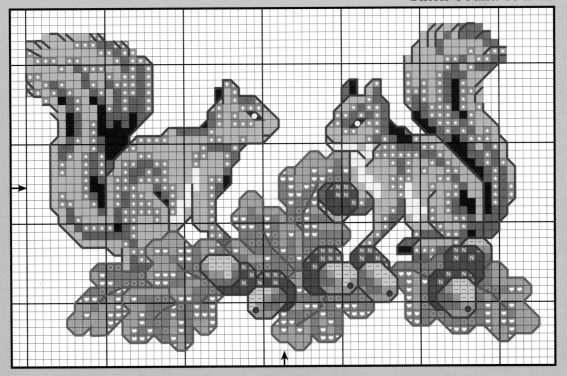

DMC = Kreinik		DMC = Kreinik		DMC = Kreinik		DMC = Kreinik	
Snow White	Blanc	367	1835/3425	554	3312	725	2514
Ecru		368	1832/1842	561	146	726	522
Creme/F2/F13		369	1841	562	144	727	2521
208	1334/3335	370	2214	563	143/211	729	
209	1342/3334	372	3833	564	141	2234/2243/2533	
210	3334	400	4141/4215	580	516	730	3724
211	3333	402	632/2622	581	2124	731	516/2214
221	4623/4624	407	4611	597	132	732	2124
223	4622	413	3445	598	1721/1723	733	2212
224	4621	414	3442	602	3014	734	2212
225	1011	415	3441	603	3013	738	3821/4112
300	4142	420	526	604	3012	739	4241
301	2625	422	3812	605	3021	740	624
304	943/1026	433	4116/4122	606	915/935	741	611/624
307	543	434	4516	608	635	742	545
309	2934/2945	435	4236	610	3835	743	536
310	Noir	436	4235	611	4534	744	2532
311	1716	437	4234	612	3833	745	2542
312	1715	444	536	613	3832	746	2541
315	4646	451	3414	632	4143	747	1723
316	4634	452	3413/3414	640	3834	754	1012
317	3445	453	3412/3413	642	3713	758	2912
318	3442	469	2125	644	3422	760	2932/2943
319	1845	470	245/2125	645	3844	761	1013/2931
320	1834	471	2114	646	3843	762	3441
321	941/943	472	2122/2123	647	1734	772	2113
322	4922	498	945/1026	648	3841	775	1441
326	1026	500	1846	666	915/935	776	2941
327	3315	501	1844/3426	676	2242	778	4631/4634
333	1344	503	1843	677	2141	780	3816/3826
334	1434	504	1822	680	524	781	2516/3825
335	3014	517	1446/1725	699	225	782	2244
336	1423	518	1444	700	226	783	2244
340	1343	519	1442	701	235	791	1345
341	1433	520	3726	702	224/236	793	4913
347	2924	522	1832/1842	703	223	794	1434
349	915/935	523	1841	704	221	796	116
350	914/934	524	3423	712	Brut	797	4924
351	924	535	3844	718	1043	798	4923
352	932/933	543	3431	720	634	799	4922
353	921/2913	550	3336/3315	721	645	800	4921
355	2636	552	3314	722	633	801	4115
356	4612	553	3313			806	126

DMC	=	Kreinik		DMC	=	Kreinik		DMC	=	Kreinik		DMC	=	Kreinik
807		125		907		244		973		536		3350		3025
809		1434		909		225		975		4215		3354		3021/3011
813		1443		910		226		976		4212		3362		3726
814		2926/4625		911		214		977		611/2546		3363		1832/1833
815		2925		913		213		986		1845		3364		1831/3723
816		946		917		1043		987		2116		3371		4136
817		916		918		4142		988		2115		3609		1312
818		2942		919		2636		989		234		3685		3026
819		1011		920		2625		991		1826		3687		3023/3024
820		116		921		2615		992		5013		3688		1042
822		3711/3811		922		644		993		1823		3689		3031
823		163/1425		924		205		995		114		3705		914/934
824		115		926		1745		996		113		3706		932
825		1446		927		1744		3011		516		3708		1021/1022
826		113		928		1742		3012		2124		3712		2914
827		1442		930		1715		3013		3722		3713		1011
828		1721		931		1714		3021		3846		3716		3021
829		526		932		1712		3022		3715		3726		4645
830		2214		934		3726		3023		3422		3727		3031
831		2214		935		2126		3024		3421/3841		3731		3013
832		2235		936		2136		3031		4115		3733		3012
833		2233		937		516		3032		4534		3743		3322
834		2242		938		4124		3033		3711		3746		1343
838		4124		939		165		3041		4635		3747		4911
839		3433		945		2632		3042		4633		3750		1716
840		3345/3434		946		634		3045		3742		3752		1712
841		3341		948		2911		3046		2231		3755		112
842		3431/4531		950		2912		3047		2541/2542		3760		1445
844		3844/3846		951		4241		3051		2126		3761		1722
869		526		954		143/211		3052		3723		3765		126
890		1836/1845		955		141		3053		3722		3766		125
891		914		956		1024		3064		4611		3768		1745
893		1014		957		1022		3072		111/1813		3770		F13
894		1022		958		5013		3078		2521		3772		4611
895		1845		959		5012		3325		4921		3774		2911
898		4131/4124		961		3013		3326		3021		3776		644
899		2933		962		3022		3328		2915		3778		2642
900		635/636		963		2942		3340		912		3779		2912
902		2926/4626		964		5011		3341		911		3787		3344
904		2116		966		142		3345		2116		3799		3445
905		224		970		634		3346		2115				
906		223		971		633		3347		2114				
				972		544/545		3348		2113				

Metric Conversion Chart

mm-millimetres cm-centimetres
inches to millimetres and centimetres

inches	mm	cm	inches	cm	inches	cm
⅛	3	0.3	9	22.9	30	76.2
¼	6	0.6	10	25.4	31	78.7
½	13	1.3	12	30.5	33	83.8
⅝	16	1.6	13	33.0	34	86.4
¾	19	1.9	14	35.6	35	88.9
⅞	22	2.2	15	38.1	36	91.4
1	25	2.5	16	40.6	37	94.0
1¼	32	3.2	17	43.2	38	96.5
1½	38	3.8	18	45.7	39	99.1
1¾	44	4.4	19	48.3	40	101.6
2	51	5.1	20	50.8	41	104.1
2½	64	6.4	21	53.3	42	106.7
3	76	7.6	22	55.9	43	109.2
3½	89	8.9	23	58.4	44	111.8
4	102	10.2	24	61.0	45	114.3
4½	114	11.4	25	63.5	46	116.8
5	127	12.7	26	66.0	47	119.4
6	152	15.2	27	68.6	48	121.9
7	178	17.8	28	71.1	49	124.5
8	203	20.3	29	73.7	50	127.0

Index